Smoke & Dust

Poems and Illustrations

Perry Scott Woodfin

Introduction

Art is something that you try to move from the inside of you, to the outside physical world. As a visual artist when I try to do this, it's usually a difficult thing to do. It can be hard to make something come alive for myself, let alone an audience, and often involves a long process of refinement where I polish an idea and the resulting object, over and over and over. On the other hand, poetry which is also a serious art form for me, often happens fast. I find it very immediate and magical the way a poem can literally leap into existence. Art has always been a fun activity for me, from childhood to today. When making a serious statement, art must have this element of play for me to remain interested and excited, or I tend to lose interest. This immediacy that poetry has for me definitely contributes to my sense of play and is often included in my visual art.

I enjoyed doing the illustrations for this book. I tried to be visually poetic and have fun at the same time. My hope is that while reading, you will too.
-Perry Scott Woodfin

FOR JUDITH WITH LOVE

Copyright

FIRST EDITION

For more information or to see more of his work,
please visit Perry's website at:
www.perrywoodfin.com

Contents

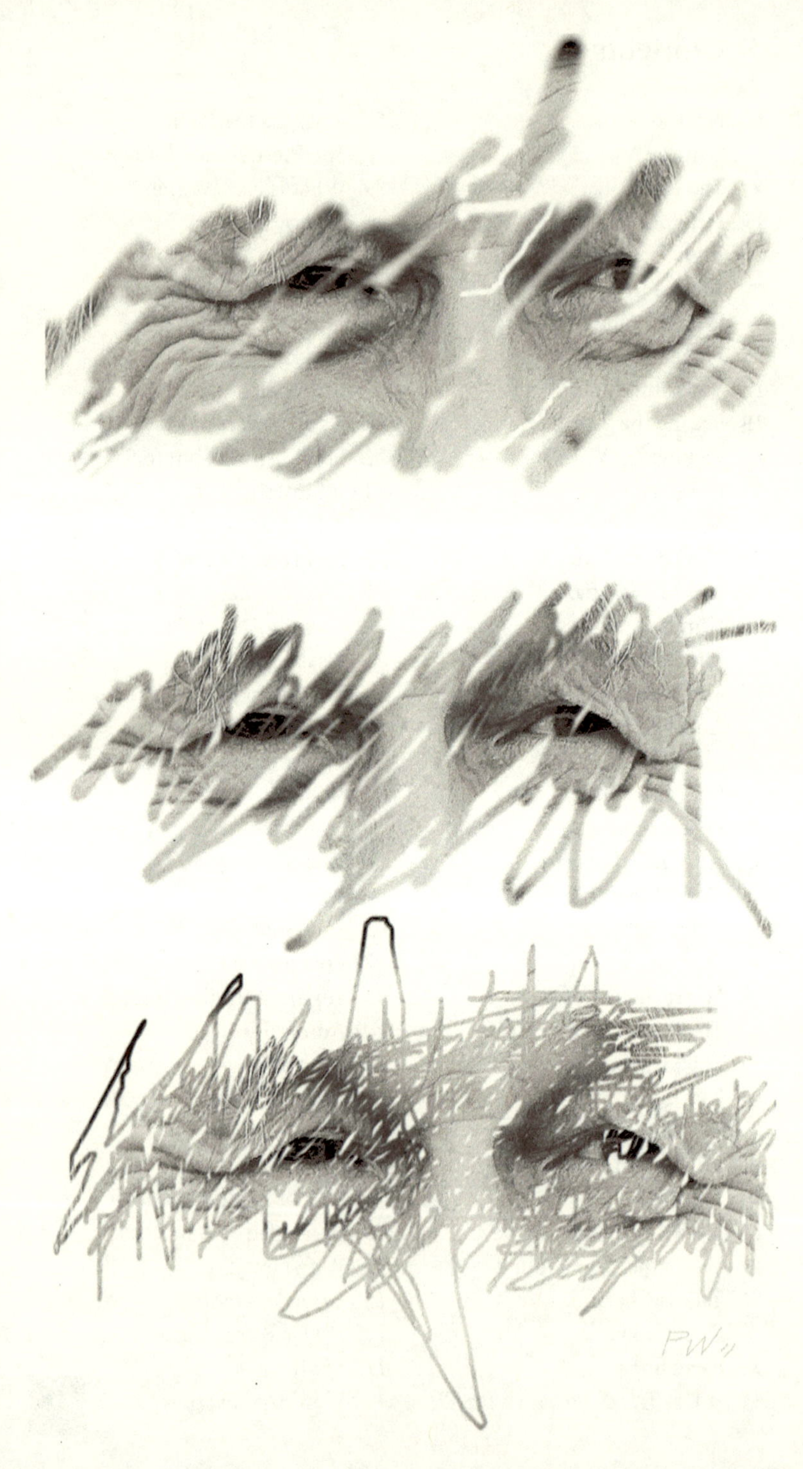

Norway

Growing up
on an island near Seattle,
the Olympic Mountains hung in the crystal air
like a whisper above dark green uncut timber.
Wavering, they promised the elusive mysteries of distance.
And blue water reflections spoke of fjords and other things.
Entranced, I was sure it was Norway.

A grown man,
I know this water is the Colvos Passage
and car fumes now mask the Olympics.
Timber is patched by clear cuts.
The old neighbors, childless Norwegians who baby sat,
have disappeared too.
Berger's heart stopped,
overworking in the fuel and oil of a ferryboat engine room
where pistons don't shut down
except by orders from the pilot above,
and Seigford, heartbroken,
sailed home on an ocean,
dying amid heavy fir
near the darkness of deep blue that never stops circulating.

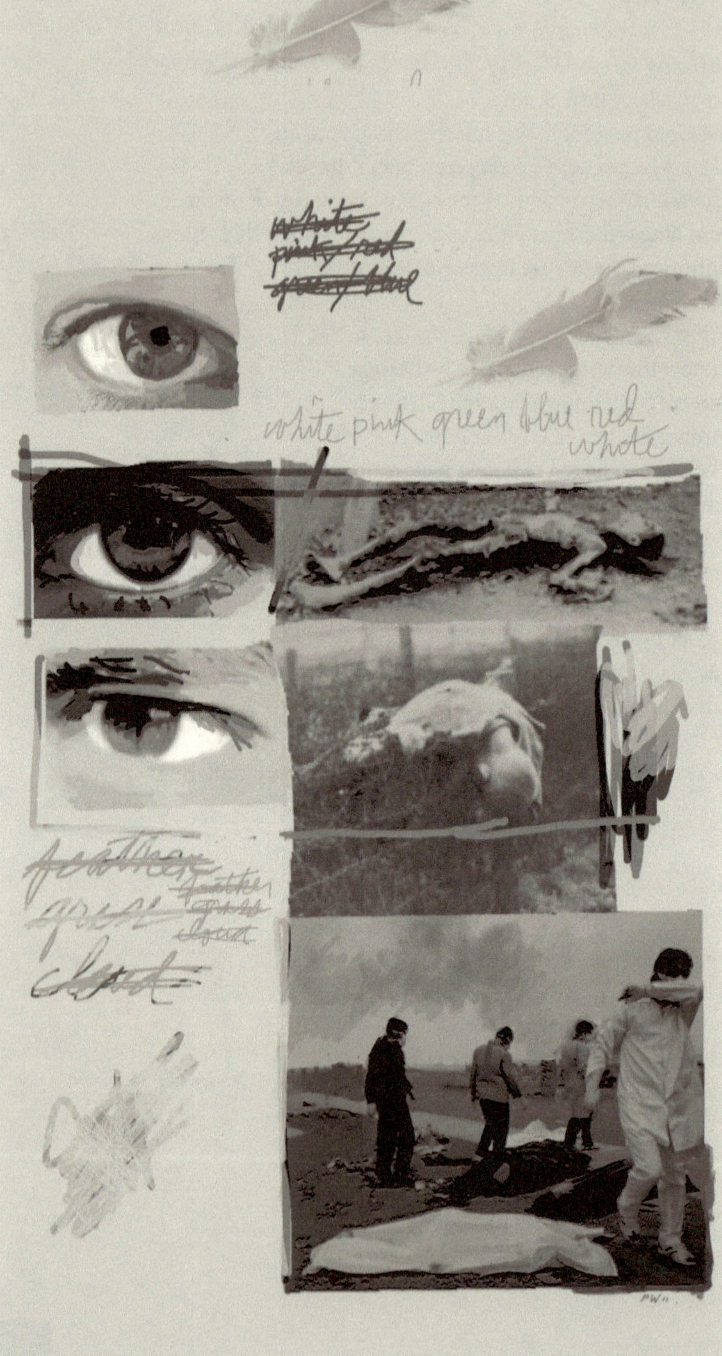
white pink green blue red
white

Spring

Right outside my window I see this large robin
singing on a blossoming apple tree limb.
The early sun is drawing shadows from his western half,
awakening his hunger for the day.
I watch his warbling and below, the grasses and weeds dance
as temperature rises, bringing on breeze.
Beyond, the water of the Sound ripples unevenly,
being swept by indiscriminate clean air.
Cumulus clouds bunch up on the horizon.
Pink blossom, red feathers, white cloud.
Green grass, blue water and more.
On the table, my radio gives me a detailed account
of a massacre that once occurred in the hills of Kosovo.
So foreign to what I see, it tells of rows of dug graves
with the fresh bodies of young men
perched above on piles of dirt, ready to slide in.
Did the eyes of these dead look out into spring groves
and see the same things I do?
Or were they blinded, earth resting on pupils,
in that black country in shadow to the east?

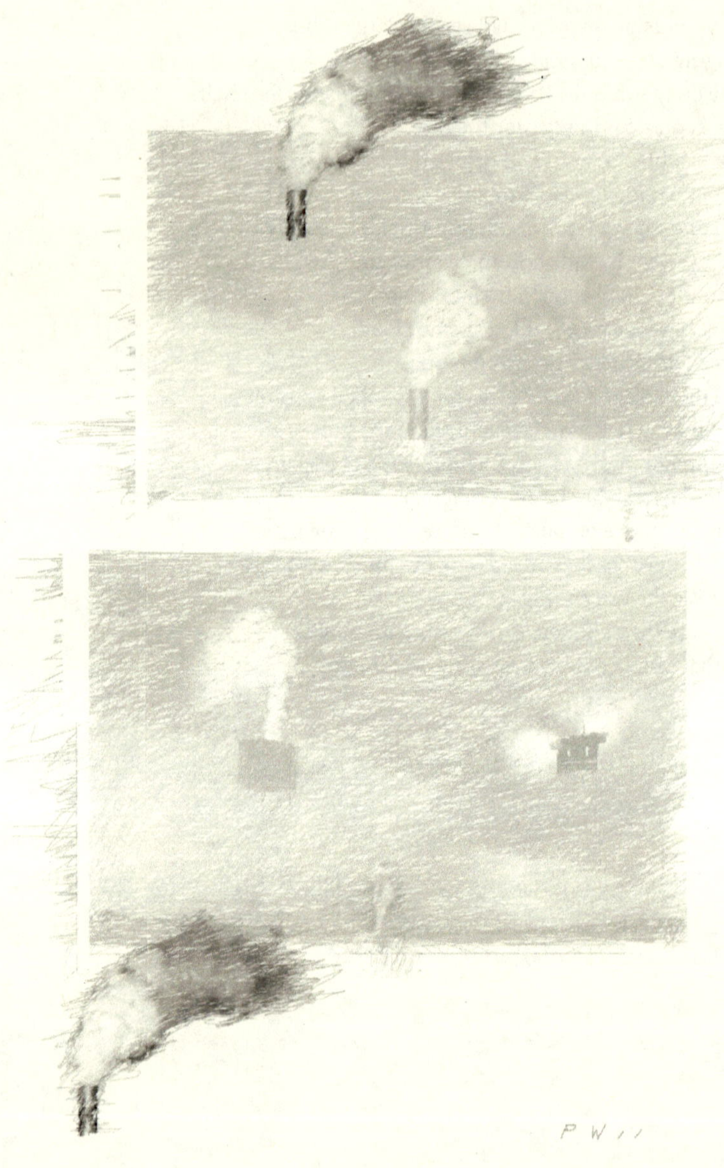

The Fall

The dogs whine, telling me they want out.
I put on their leashes, take them out, tie them and go back in.
Rain begins and it is a serious rain.
Not hard, but the kind you know will last
with heavy drops that mean something.
When they hit, their pitter-patter seems to come right through.
It chills me but makes me comfortable too, warm next to the wood stove.
The dogs whine again, this time to get back in.
Getting them, the wind whips at me and I look up.
Up on the hill the hay has long been gathered
and is drying inside weathered old barns.
People try to do most of their work inside now.
This squall is signaling that this is just the start;
that there is more coming in the months ahead.
The neighbor's fire lights up and the smoke shoots off horizontally
as soon as it clears the chimney.
It joins the heavy clouds being driven down from Alaska,
sailing east off the strait.
Moisture and soot, this gray hungers for the mountains, the continent.
Time will lengthen now, fed by the wind, the rain, and the smoke.
It's what winter grows on.

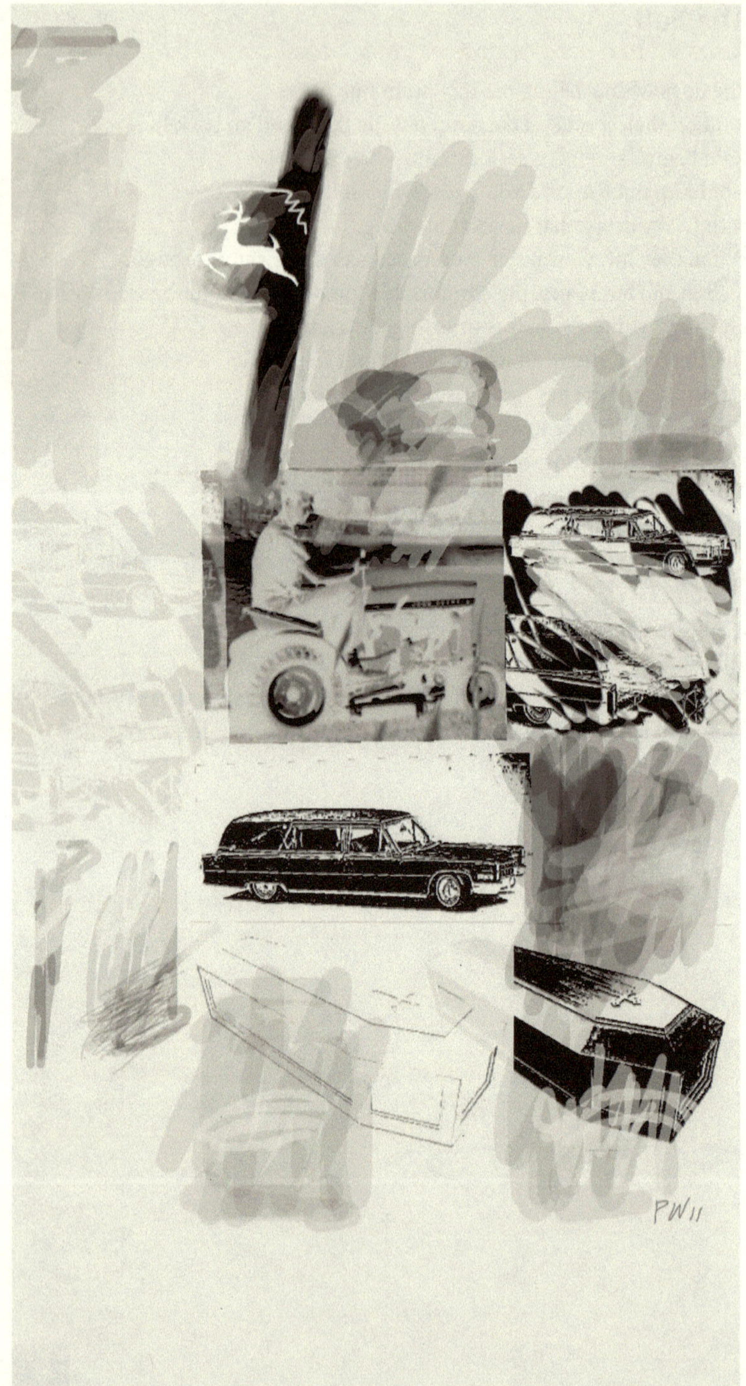
PW11

Dead Ringer

Today, a funeral procession went driving by,
one car after another, after another.
Everyone's lights were on, all following the hearse.
It was a big old Cadillac with a coffin riding in back.
Ostentatious, authoritarian, auspicious.
Who are they kidding, heading for that grave like follow the leader?
They'll get there sooner. Or later.
Got me thinking about my death, death's door dead ahead.
Can't escape it. It's like a deadline
where I'm the project that's going to be due.
As they say: It could happen anywhere, anytime.
Nowhere to run. I see it. I'm ready.
So here and now let me say I would prefer cremation.
Let's get it down on record.
Would much rather go up in smoke and dust
than take up space, someone mowing grass over me.
Probably on a John Deere too or some kind of riding lawnmower.
Don't believe in it. Uses too much oil and gas.
Just let the grass grow, for God's sake.
Use me as fertilizer if you want.
Grass could always be greener.
But I better not hear you didn't party. Didn't have a good time.
I want you to dance to good music until you're dead on your feet.
And I don't want any monument. No marker either.
Would be nice if you read this though.
And thought about that part of you I take with me.
Can you remember?

Stamping Ground

I rack my brain,
hanging on every word
crossing my mind
like a steel trap
chained to letters
sent anonymously.

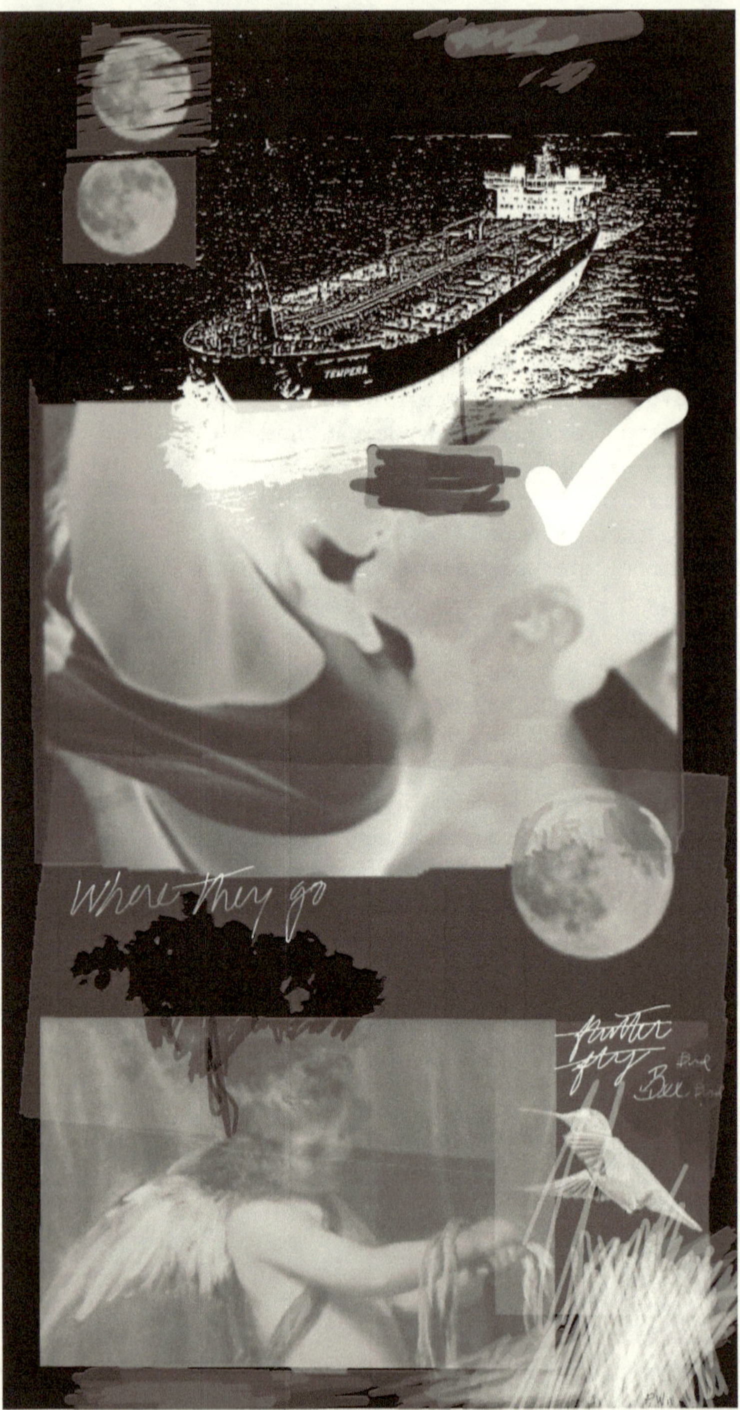
TEMPERA
Where they go

In the Same Boat

Where do they go when it's cold?
Hummingbirds in early spring
must have a hard time of it.
Do they gather the heat
that hovers over energetic lovers?
He thought he'd heard it, its sound,
its telltale wings fluttering,
fluttering fast, and wondered.
Their feet were dangling off
the high cliff above the Strait,
with its ships prowing
toward Alaska or the Orient,
when he heard the buzzing
and hesitating, mentioned it to her.
It was so early though.
They couldn't believe it.
Deep into their own song high
on the bluff over crashing ocean,
their leap of faith in birds 'n bees
excerpted the birds.
Continuing like nothing happened,
his hand dove through her clothes
like a bow parting water.

Subdue

The bed, vacant,
wants.
It throws covers.
Strips sheets.
Rising sun's flame
moves surface.
Back and forth
flesh-like rumples
collide in mirror
floor to ceiling
doubling up
blanket skin
like a memory
and gives itself away.
Vacant bed springs
whenever I look at it
seeing you.

Winter of Discontent

Spring chicken laid an egg!
Fall from grace
killed goose with golden egg
in one fell swoop.
An out of season stoning
of two birds with one failure.

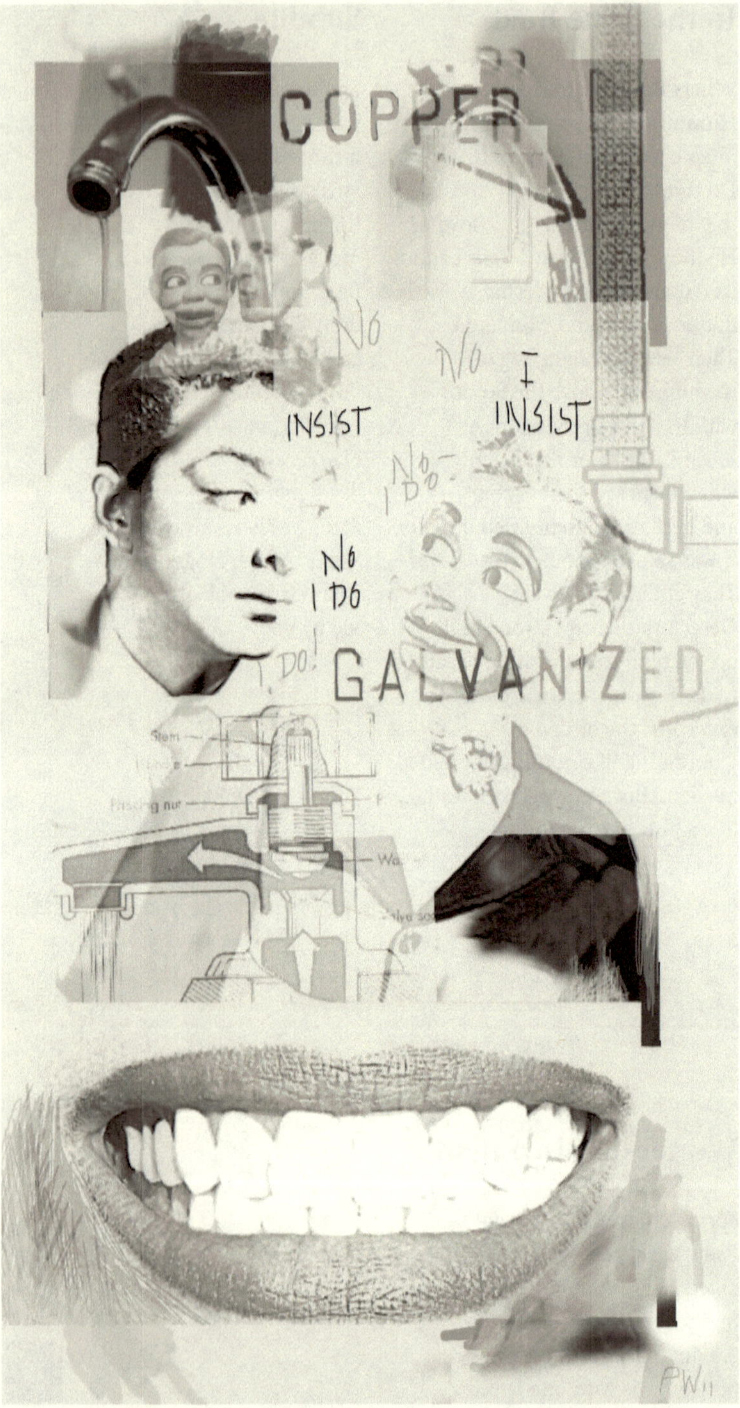
COPPER
No
No
I
INSIST
INSIST
No
I DO
No
I DO
I DO!
GALVANIZED
Stem
PW11

Fluent

The water dripped from the faucet
and for a long time I fought with it,
trying to make it stop
because it started to really get to me
with its drip, drip, dripping on
the surface of the enameled white
black cast iron sink, but unable to,
I personified it
and it became insistent
saying I was wasteful,
wasting its preciousness,
and why couldn't I make it stop,
over and over until finally
after the longest period of time
I relaxed
so that the pressure lessened
and my futility at handling it
just poured out of me,
each drop, dropping away
and I could see that
I'd stood at that sink
and in my frustration
heard a mistaken tongue
whose attack I'd thought
was rhythmically stressful
and now, suddenly,
I understood
that I was a ventriloquist
and the constant murmuring
piped down.

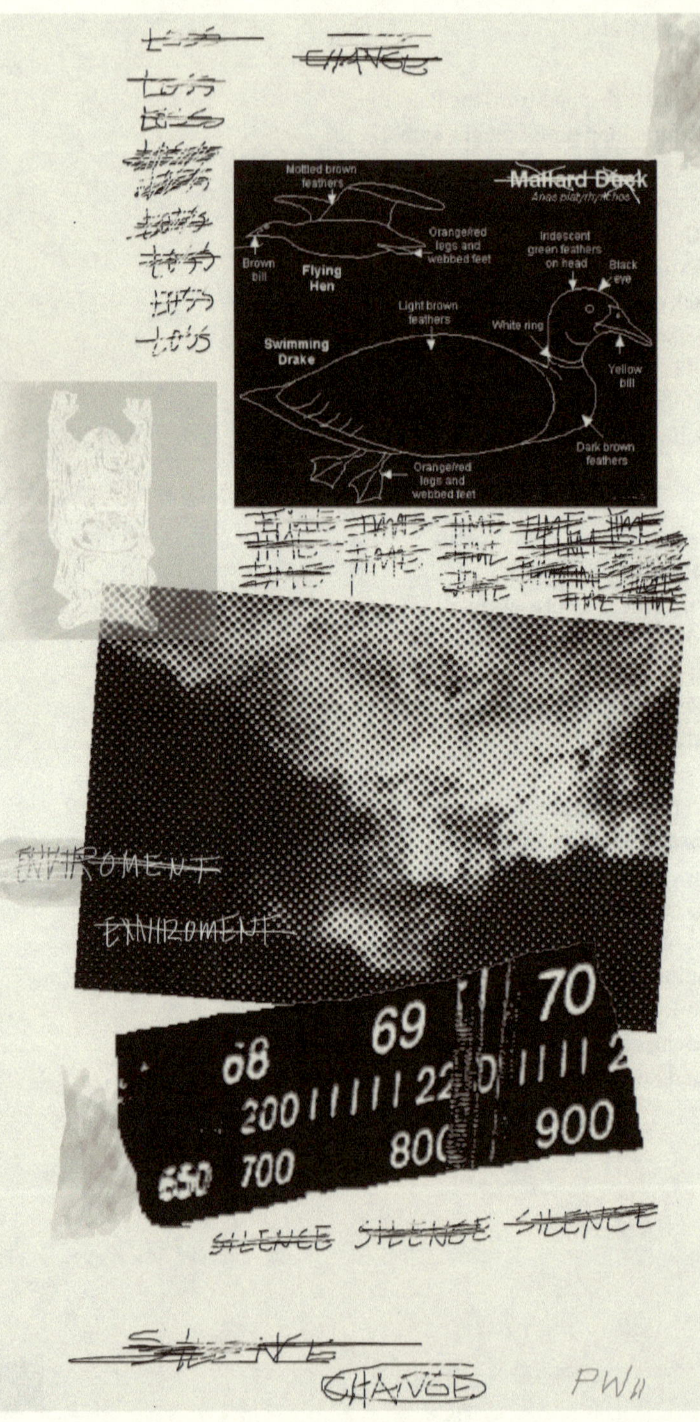
CHANGE
Mottled brown feathers
Mallard Duck
Anas platyrhynchos
Orange/red legs and webbed feet
Iridescent green feathers on head
Brown bill
Flying Hen
Black eye
Light brown feathers
White ring
Swimming Drake
Yellow bill
Dark brown feathers
Orange/red legs and webbed feet
TIME TIME TIME TIME TIME
ENVIROMENT
ENVIROMENT
70
69
68
200
900
800
700
650
SILENCE SILENCE SILENCE
SILENCE
CHANGE
PW

Vicissitude

Lost in thought, it doesn't stand a chance.
Before I know it, the morning news flies by.
As is my custom, I sip my coffee, looking out at the cove.
A solitary mallard disappears.
Where's the flock, its partner?
Aren't they bonded together for life?
All this conjures up the past year. It went so fast.
One year ago today Jeanette lost her life.
I remember. It was sunny.
Not like today. Today the air is heavy.
Thick clouds are driven by a stiff mean biting wind.
In the distance, blue patches appear, then disappear.
They testify that there really is a summer somewhere.
But it's cold here, really cold, almost stormy.
Poppies she planted, her poppies, pop out of the green.
They're bright flashes of red.
Nice, but poor substitutes for the sun I miss.
Out a week or less, their fragile thin petals fade.
They fall away. Small seeds scatter, like ground pepper lost.
The ground is fertilized for next year with a colored carpet of light
and I'm left here rushing headlong toward who knows what.
That's how I feel today. Uncertain.
Life shifts about like the neighboring weather vane.
First here, then there.
Her death, desultory, willed me constant grief at first.
Overwhelming.
Then the grief spasmodically appeared.
Now it just sits waiting for occasions like this.
For occasions when a lone duck flies by.
Meanwhile, crowding all around me are silly objects.
Like this stool I built real fast one day.
The chipped plates on the shelf.
That small replica of Buddha standing and laughing in the corner.
They just make me question what stays and what leaves.
Jeanette, full of life, as colorful as the poppies, moves on.
It's the inconsequential that remains.
They hang like the gray clouds.
I see them and I just can't forgive them for that.

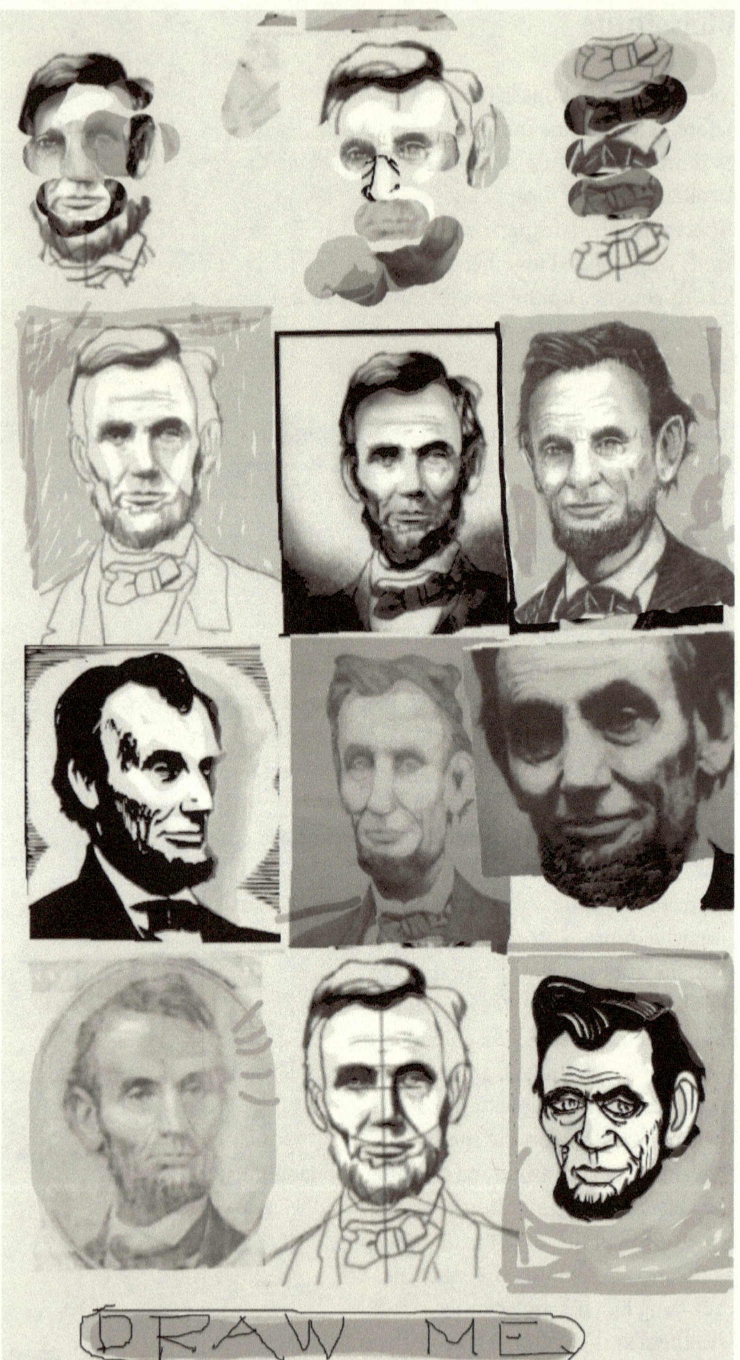
DRAW ME
PW11

Setting the World on Fire

The kid closed the match book.
Turning it in his fingers,
a drawing of Abraham Lincoln stared at him.
Draw Me, it declared
underneath in neat type.
Flicking the cover open explained
how you could become a famous artist
behind rows of matches.
Just draw me and send your money, it said,
so we can determine if you have the right stuff.
The kid wanted that; to know if he was good.
He'd do it! They'd see! He'd be so good, they'd see it right off.
He drew and folded Abe, stuffing it in an envelope with his money.
Laid it in the mailbox by the road
like it was part of him that was being sent away.
Weeks later a car pulled up. The kid was mowing the yard.
The man driving asked if he was the one who'd sent the drawing.
He was wearing a necktie and a suit.
Drove all the way down from Spokane, he said impressively.
Wanted to talk with his parents and him.
Inside, this man tried to talk them into signing up
their kid for this correspondence course.
Easy to see the kid's potential, he said to them.
Too young. Maybe when he's older, they said.
Sure made the kid feel famous though,
strange people driving up asking him if he was him and all.
Him! This kid who closed the covers to match books.
Didn't want to get burned or anything.

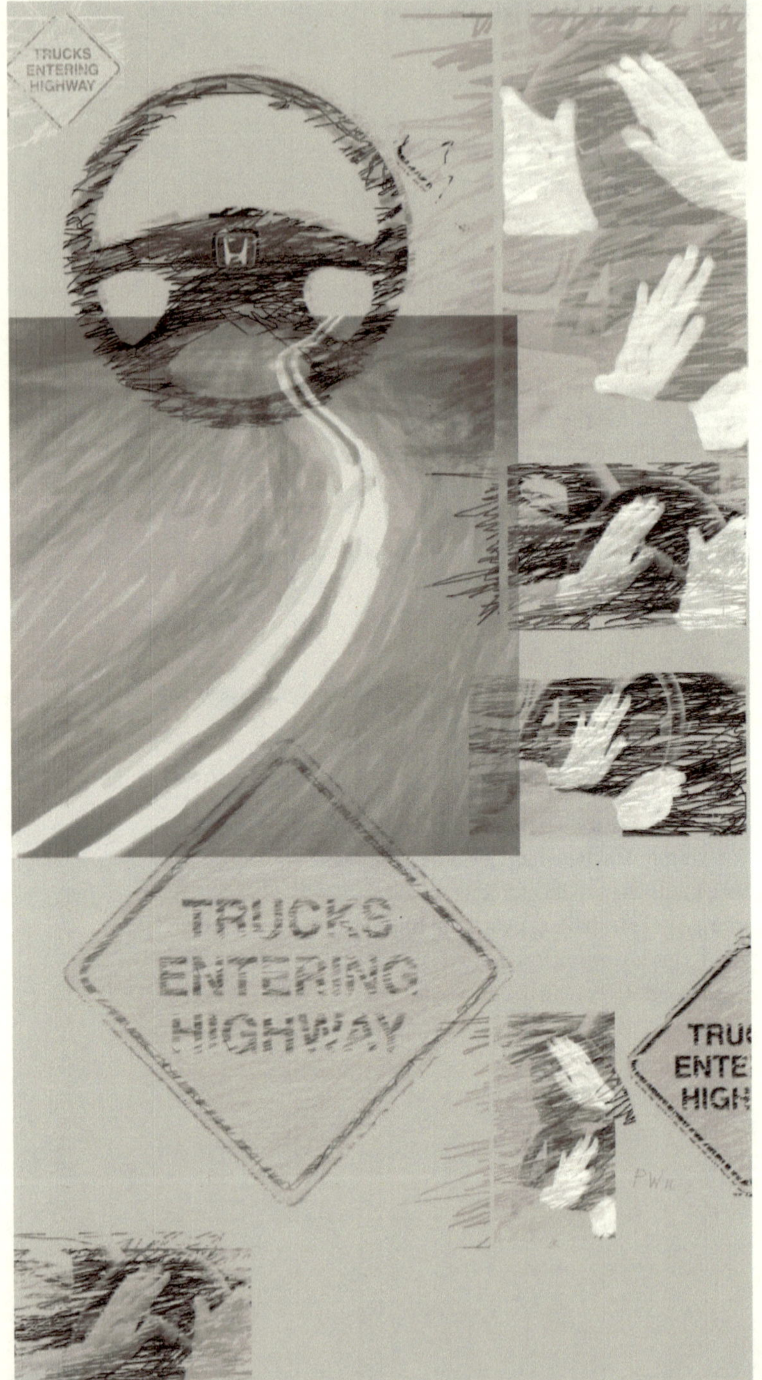
TRUCKS
ENTERING
HIGHWAY
TRUCKS
ENTERING
HIGHWAY

Picking Up Vibes

Fill up with strong coffee.
Jump in car and head out.
Moving along real good
with radio on loud
to hear over engine noise.
Play jazz.
Really get into it.
Get into long riffs and all.
Ad lib on steering wheel,
slapping it to beat the band.
Pretty soon anticipate,
leading melody with percussion.
Beauty of it all sends me real good.
We're doing great -
this band and me.
Really dig scene.
Top one song off
with couple smart honks on horn.
A salute.
Guy in front gives me finger.
Apparently
audience not paying attention.
For Christ's sake.
Just trying to have fun.
Tough on us musicians out here.

Moved

When I look up
her tears are falling.
Without much time
we kiss, touch gently.
At the gate we part
walking backward
away from each other
waving, throwing kisses,
not wanting to disappear.
Walking down the corridor,
her tears travel with me.
They touch my heart
and my soul unsuspecting,
swells, making room.
Settled, I look out
at the blacktop tarmac
knowing I carry her.
Nothing will remove her.
We lift with a strong thrust
but I'm stirred already.
Now high over the city
silver drops on the window
join those that shimmer
down her cheeks,
wondering if time
will slow again.

For Gary Wanzer

Darkness has fallen.
Birds have gone where they go.
It's quiet and melancholy arrives.
To believe Gary is gone
Is hard to arrive at.
It doesn't set in.
I look up and the moon is shining
Through closed windows.

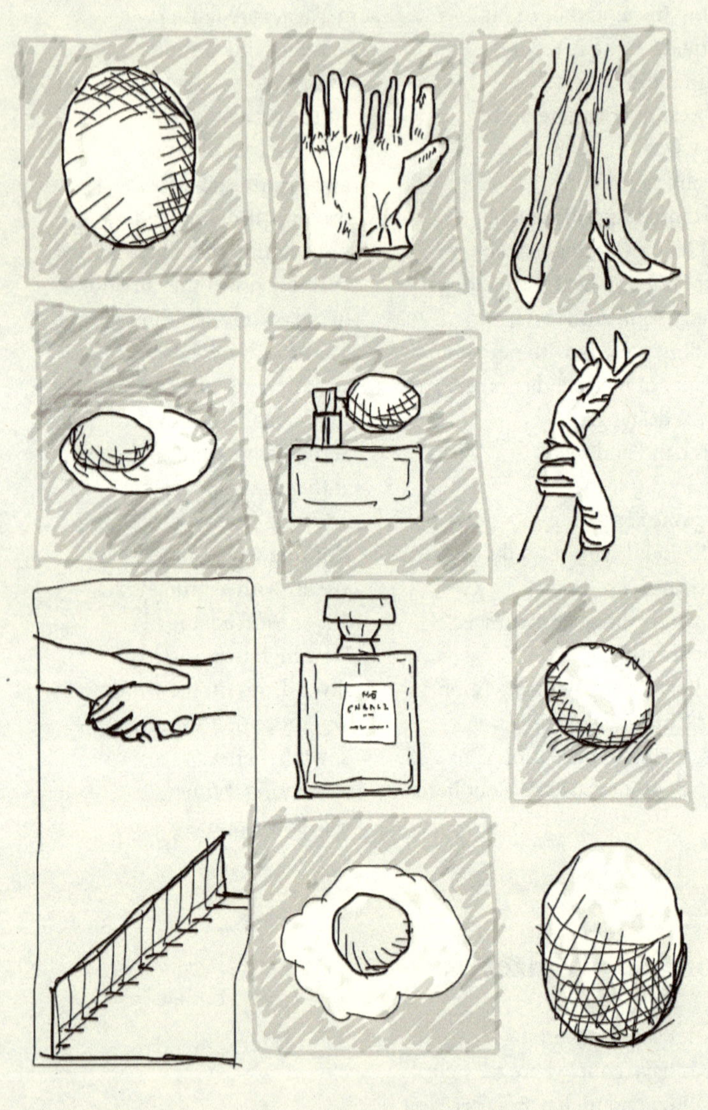

PW 11

The Egg and Me

When her name comes up, as it has on occasion,
I reminisce about our only meeting.
We had climbed the long flight to the ferry boat cabin.
We stop suddenly at the top.
A woman is coming down.
Dad and Mom talk with her.
Dad, proud, introduces me, his boy.
Then he tells me, "This is Betty MacDonald."
To me she's just another grown up.
I seem to remember all of that.
I think she had on silk stockings, high heels.
There may also have been white gloves, perfume.
I wonder if I've invented all this?
It's just a memory, a brief moment in time.
As I said, on occasion it has come up.
Then I turn it over, move it around,
gaining nothing except what is here.
Well, maybe a slight scent of sophistication;
maybe a touch of class.
But have I hatched this too ?
Questions remain as questions always seem to do,
just laying there.
Whenever I catch a ferry and see that high flight,
small memories like this, soar.

Loud Love Affair

A love game
on lovers' lane
at the top of lungs
bursting at their seams -
no love lost
for crying out loud.

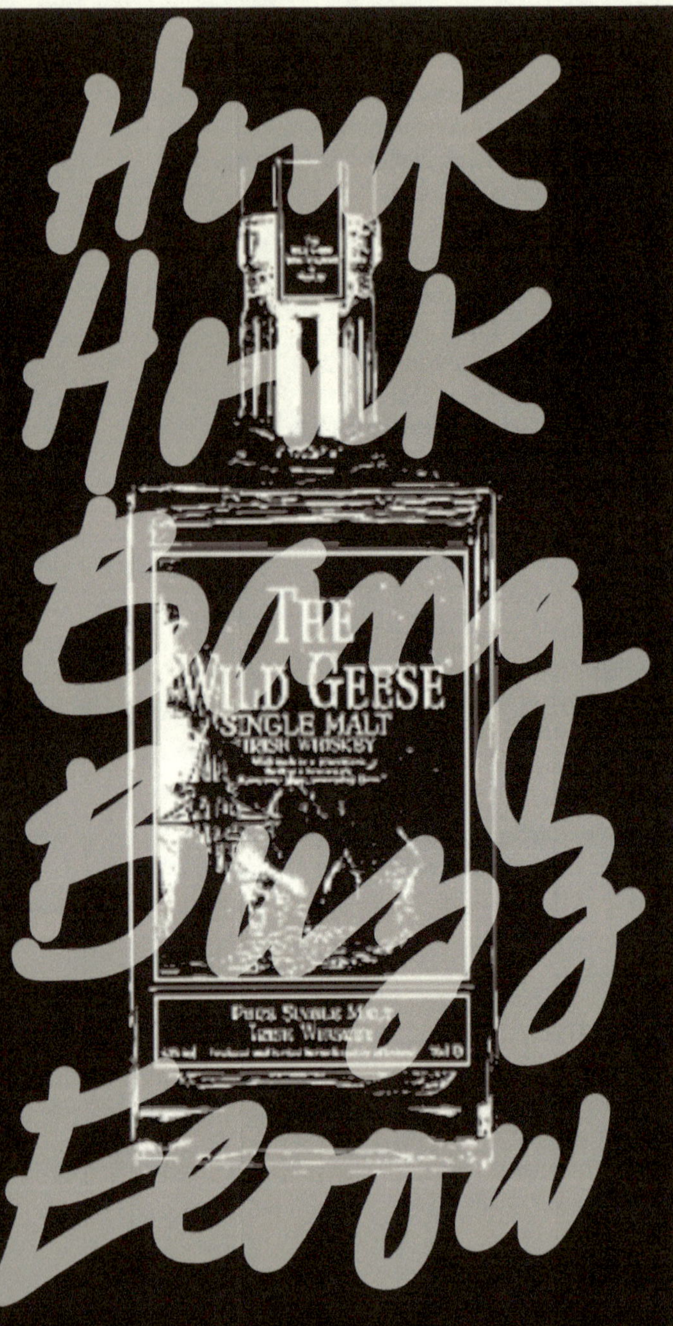
Honk
Honk
Bang
Bang
THE
WILD GEESE
SINGLE MALT
IRISH WHISKEY

Numbed

The sun parts the clouds
and I can see blue sky again.
The minute it does,
November's deadening, like magic,
lessens and slows.
The wind's whispering
stills in all directions.
It allows the honking of a lone wild goose
to push through, echoing
between the old uneven glass panes
and the faded lace curtains.
Hunters' shotguns haven't got it yet,
but, given time, they will.
The clouds come again.
In here, warmed air produces a buzzing.
A fly, arriving late, just as suddenly, disappears.
It seems like it was only yesterday
when I would have driven
all of this out with my own call:
Eeoow! Come on! Let's drink!
Come on, drink up for God's sake!
Can't we have a little fun?
Let's drink and just forget ourselves.

Live Artist

I brushed up
on painting
myself into a corner.
Did a good job too.
Now I can select
a pretty frame
of mind
and call it a day.
What a luxurious life.

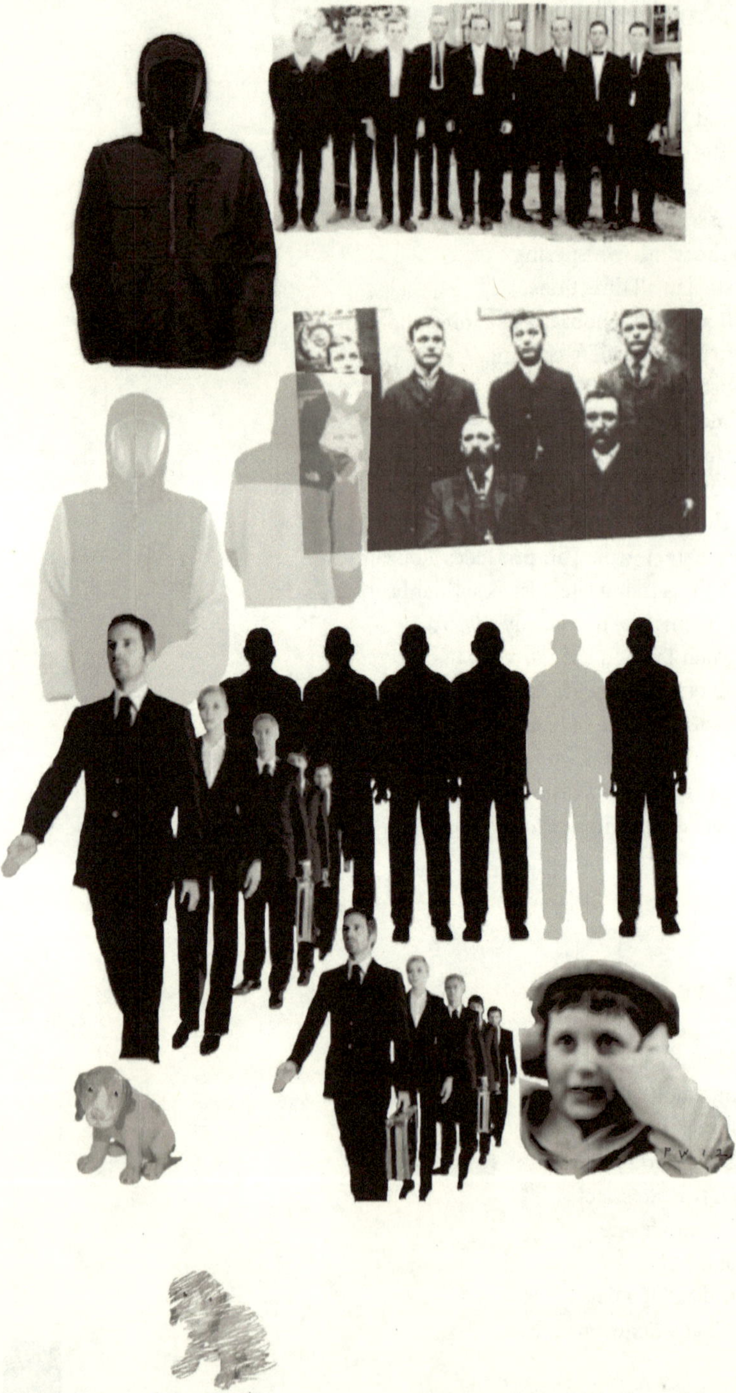

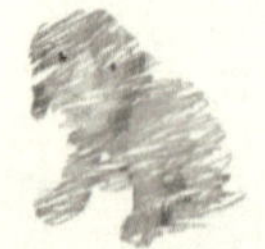

The Porcelain Dog

A long time ago, in another place not far from here,
as a small boy I had nightmares where things literally chased me
around my bed, up in this large full length attic where I slept -
if terror in that deep dark can be called sleep.

Not wanting to spoil me, my parents would say good night,
turn off the light, and hope I'd be all right, but all that did was signal me
that I could begin dreading those things that I knew waited
in the blackness of the corner closet or just under my bed.

Then they brought in an expert who suggested to them
that they put something up there with me that I could focus on,
and that would draw my attention and beguile me into forgetting
about those other things that lay there hiding out of sight.

To this day I remember the small ceramic dog, green eyes glowing,
sitting obediently on the shelf at night for me and me alone,
always watching my heavy eyes tire and drop with comforting sleep,
as I rehearsed over and over the knowledge that someone really cared.

Afterwords

Sometime I'll sit down and read all that I've written.
I think I know what I'll say.
I'll say there's so much I haven't said. Really.
There's so much I haven't gotten into.
I'll say, of course, it's all been said by writers who I envy.
I envy them just by reading them.
They say it so much better than I can.
Why then, must I?
I'll say this and the words will spring to life as if born of themselves.
Maybe I'll have forgotten this.
Will they provoke me then;
provoke me into silence,
into not writing something...
like this?

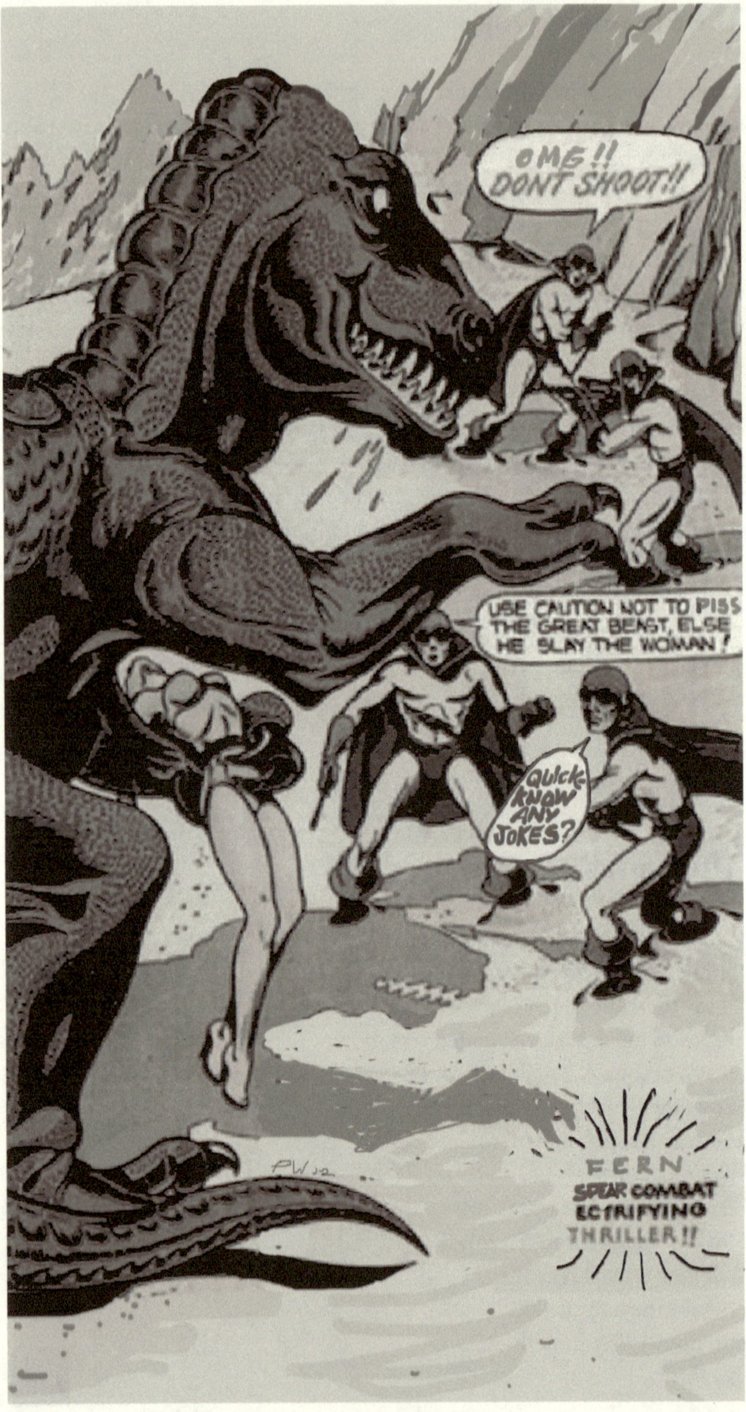

OMG!!
DONT SHOOT!!
USE CAUTION NOT TO PISS THE GREAT BEAST, ELSE HE SLAY THE WOMAN!
QUICK-KNOW ANY JOKES?
FERN
SPEAR COMBAT
ECTRIFYING
THRILLER!!

The Flash of Wit

A place of quiet, that small gentle valley.
Fern covered, it spreads green out into moist clean air.
Fern stalks make perfect spears that when thrown,
rustle leaves that sparkle, kissing each other in late afternoon sun.
Three boys toss them at imagined targets,
anything but quiet after a school day of reading and writing.
Everything is still a game they have fun at, sharpening by testing.
Talk of girls turns their conversation, each trying to act
more mature and wiser than the other two.
They walk, wading through the waist high ferns
getting into territory they haven't covered before.
A slight breeze softens everything, moving undergrowth
as if large snakes slithered around down there.
They throw their weapons at their imaginations
with the words from one tempting out those of the next.
Single file in this jungle, one suddenly tells
the first dirty joke any of them has heard,
and they laugh pretending they knew
what they would do if they had a girl.
Swish! Ferns part the still air and leaves tremble.
Without their knowing, their target is much larger.

Imitating Life

In 1950 I would have given anything for a Roy Rogers outfit
but a friend received it instead while I got some Gene Autry chaps
and as fate would have it, both of us, wearing these the same day,
were grabbed by schoolmates who seized the opportunity to circle
and spur us on as Gene and Roy wrestling in the dirt, dust flying,
until suddenly, the principal's red face appeared close yelling
for us to stop acting like children. He grabbed and shook us.

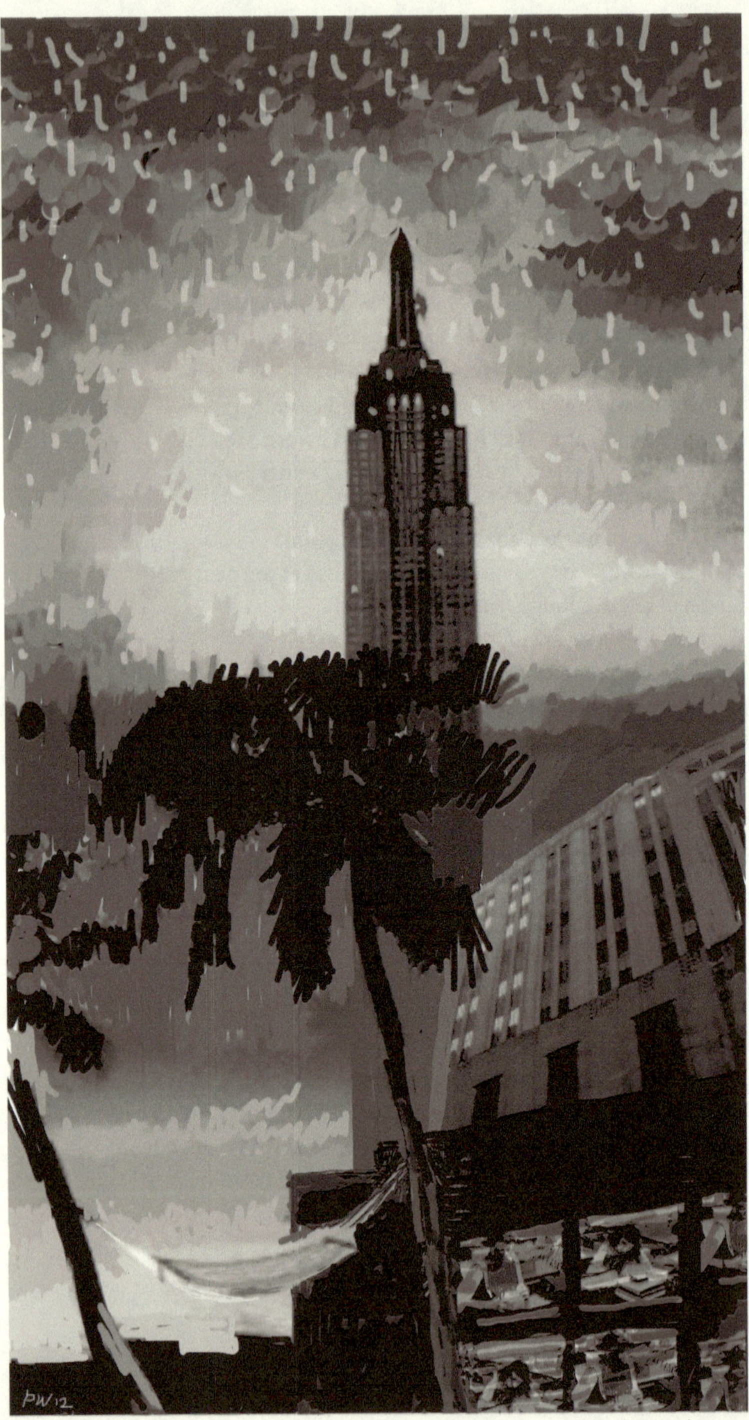
PW'12

Lost Empire

It rings three times or more before I answer it.
Hello.
Is this Perry? an older woman asks.
Yes.
Perry, I don't know if you'll remember - I'm Florence Smith.
You mean my third grade teacher?
You remember! You were always such a nice boy. Listen.
I'm retired and I'm traveling around looking up all my favorite pupils.
I'm in New York. Can I come over?
I look out the window into the airshaft.
It's a little bit of space surrounded by offices, Empire State Building nearby.
I can see secretaries typing away, shuffling paper.
Heavy snow begins falling. It falls faster.
It piles up on the iron of the fire escapes, the window sills.
It coats everything, making things clean, hiding the dirt.
I see Mrs. Smith in my mind. It's 1950 again.
She's standing in front of the blackboard telling us about South America.
She talks about the heat and moisture of the jungle.
For an eight year old, it sounds mysterious. I want to go there.
She has us draw what we think it looks like.
I draw and color palm trees, monkeys and a hammock.
I picture myself an explorer, lost in the vastness of the Amazon.
Collecting our drawings, Mrs. Smith holds mine up in front of the class.
Then she pins it to the bulletin board, making me feel like an artist.
I've carried that scene around with me. It's never left my mind.
The snow isn't stopping as I hang on the phone.
Huge flakes wipe out the view of those offices, those people killing time.
They cloud up everything.
They make things seem endless and not so crowded together.
How could I convey all this to my third grade teacher?
Can Mrs. Smith possibly understand what I'm feeling right now?
I'd love to see you, I say.
Still the artist, I'm hoping she won't be disappointed.

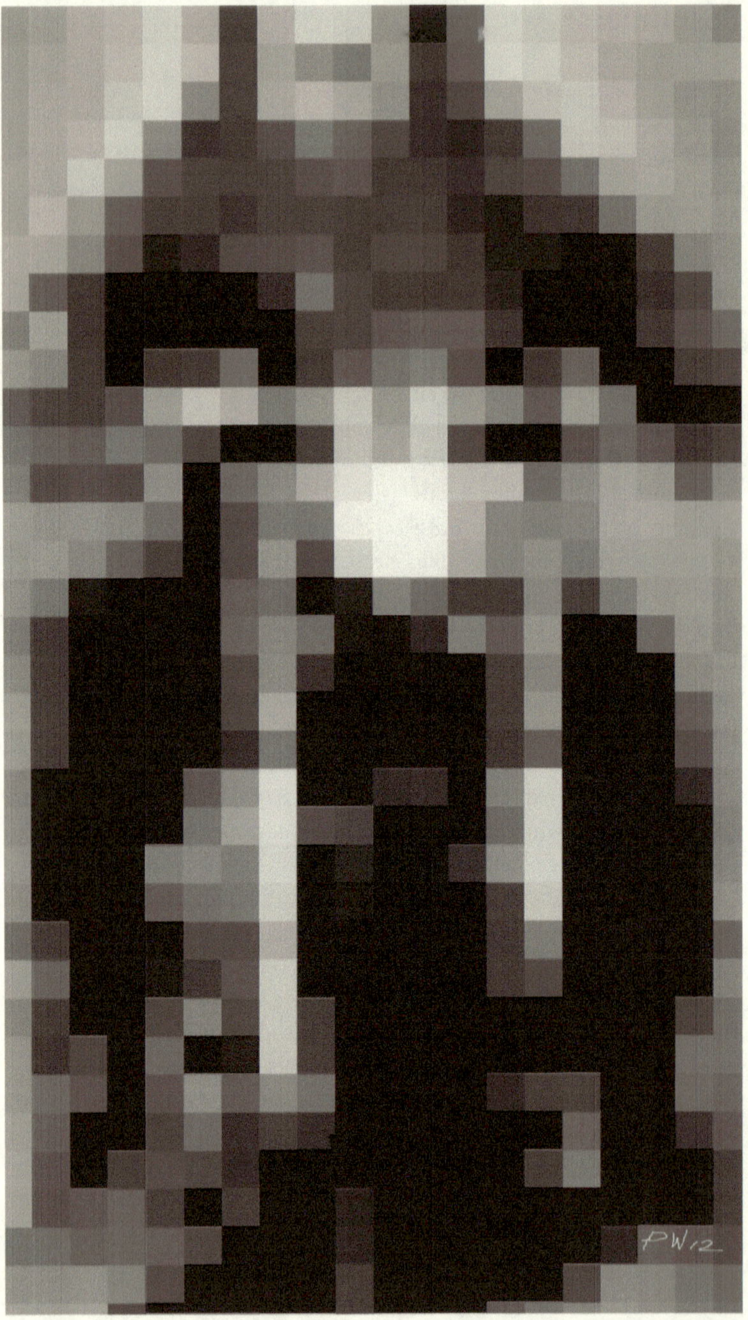
PW12

After Low Pressure

Usually after serious doubts,
I see things other people do
that also raise questions.
Strange to walk along the beach,
dogs running ahead in the sun,
soft breeze blowing, and see men
out in the blue water of the cove
doing nothing but loud circles
in - what do they call them -
personal water craft?
Heard someone call them that.
On the road over the bluff
a teenager revs a motorcycle
while his dog barks at him.
He does about sixty
to the top of the hill,
turns around and comes back.
Repeats it over and over,
and - in a racing outfit?
Someone in an SUV goes by.
Bass speakers are cranked up.
Vibrates household things loose.
The traffic is incessant.
And this is the countryside?
What is everyone doing?

Listening

I dive in
and swim to you
through the phone line.

Your sounds lure;
they promise charms
under heavy breath.

Deep down
I can't resist;
call me the catch of the day.

Desire

My Romance,
Let's Dance,
In Trance,
And Out of Pants!

Novel Illness

Writer's cramp, cramped his style.
An offhand write-off, it closed the book
wrenching the fickle fingers of fate.
He just couldn't twist language
around his little finger
and so twiddled his thumbs,
giving words body English.

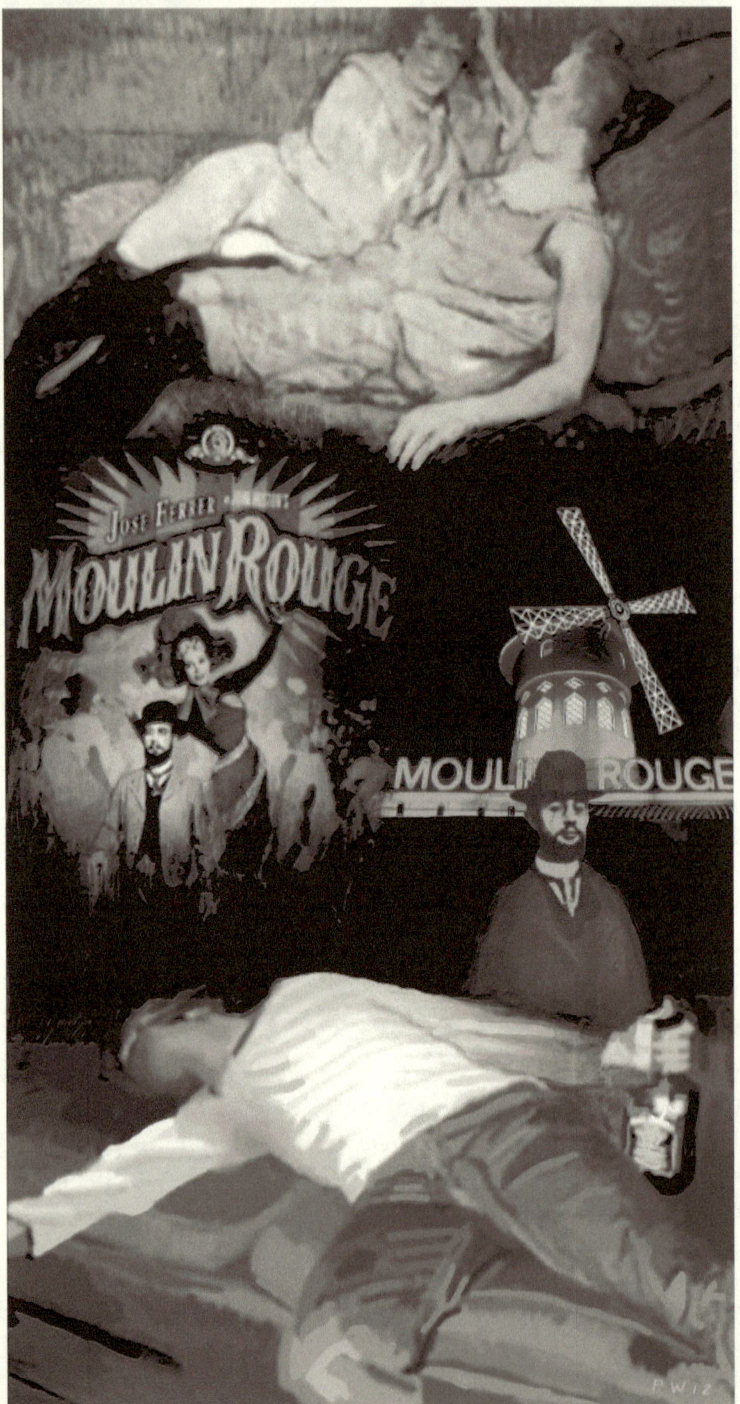
JOSE FERRER
MOULIN ROUGE
MOULI
ROUGE
P W 12

You're So Out of It

You don't know what up is.
You've been down a long time, getting messed up and all.
Smoking and drinking, you have little control over your life.
You think it would be interesting to completely lose it.
You've spiraled down a little at a time, gradual so you couldn't tell.
Now you don't do much of anything except party hard with street people.
You saw them out there sleeping in cars, fogging windows.
This one time you invited one in.
He turned around, told the others, and before you knew it, it was a party.
After that, heading to the store on the corner to pick up another bottle,
word would get out and there they were again.
Now you're resigned to it. You expect them.
Recognize who's there and who's not. Disappoints you if one is missing.
You know them by name now.
They consider you one of them and you laugh a lot, having fun.
At least you think you do. You're the artist.
They're pimps, prostitutes, and addict-thieves.
You sketch them thinking of Toulouse Lautrec.
Wonder if he got caught up in the action too; wonder if he lost days.
Sandy, a prostitute, sits across from you, wanting you to draw her.
Smiles. Smiles and then starts crying.
She's losing her looks and she needs money.
The others look away.
A crack pipe is lit.
Everyone stares, waiting for their hit, licking lips nervously in anticipation.
You drink beer. You smoke joint.
You think this could be the Moulin Rouge.
You don't even think about food, so your stomach starts eating itself.
It's fed up with you.
The alcohol burns. You're nodding. Your falling head wakes you.
You see Sandy pull her top down.
She laughs loudly, completely uninhibited.
Next morning you wake slumped alone on the table.
The smell of the cigarette butts and flat beer overcomes you.
In the bathroom, lipstick rests on the toilet and you remember her laugh.
Sounded like an animal howling in the night.
When they make the movie, Jose Ferrer can play you.
A perfect picture of debauchery and self-mastery.

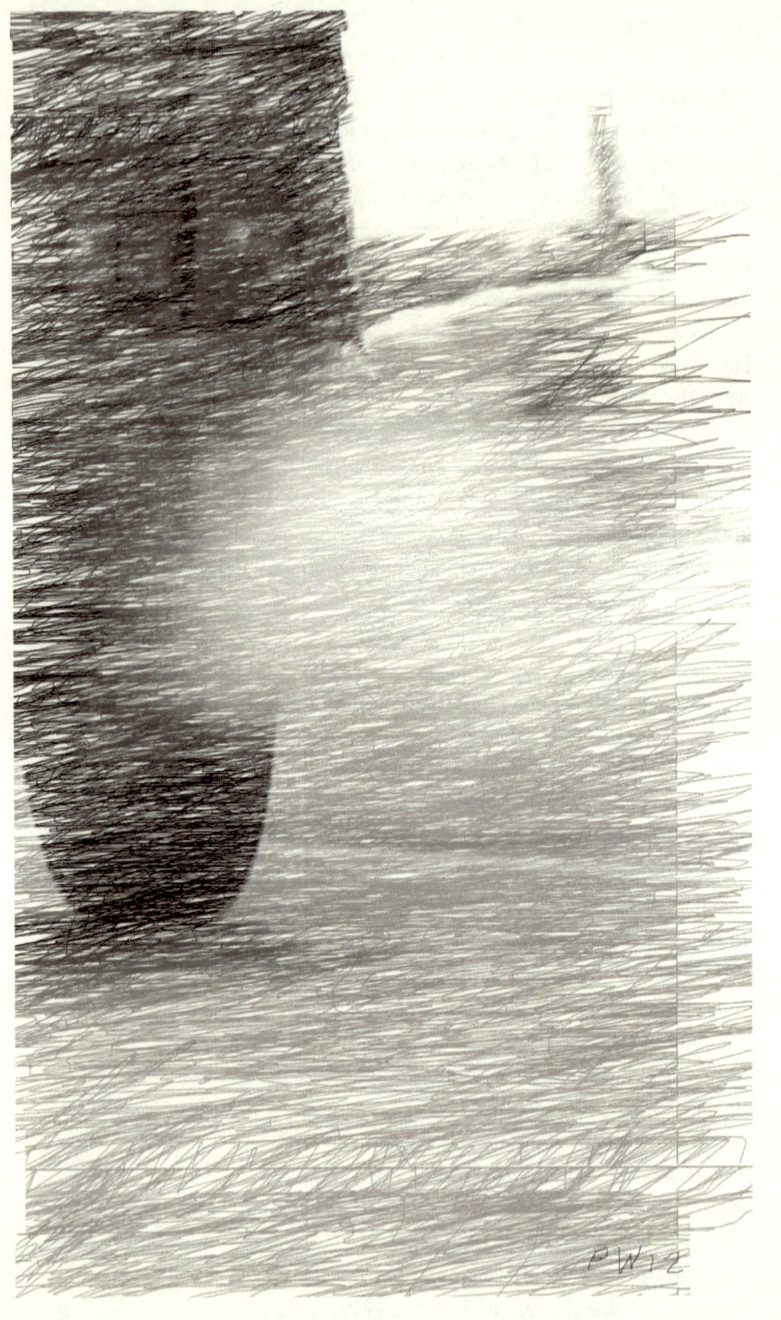

The Rabbit-foot Trance

Now and then something brushes against us.
It causes pause.
Happened again, early this morning.
Walking dogs along Penn Cove Road,
alone with wild things,
everything was quiet; peaceful.
Our minds were on our own separate things,
drifting along, waking.
Here and there rabbits jumped back into thickets
sensing us - a human,
some canines lunging on their leashes.
Hares have lousy eyesight.
Don't even see the gliding bald eagles.
Relying on ears,
they know nearby songbirds won't hurt them.
But what about the circling raptors who rip out guts as they eat?
Across the warming blacktop
we follow the snails leaving mucus trails.
They are as unaware of speeding rubber and steel as us.
Whoosh!
It soared by inches from my shoulder with an absolute warning,
causing immediate involuntary cursing
and adrenaline raised consciousness.
Shaken, I watched this shiny thing fly down the winding road.
Too fast, I didn't catch the Washington license plate number.
It was a new pick-up, a polished toy driven by a young man
intent on not allowing this guy and his dogs an inch or two.
Fierce and obviously inflexible, he nearly killed us.
It probably didn't make a dent on him.
Looking down, I saw the dogs didn't notice either.
Me?
I'm writing poetry about death
hovering over all of us all the time.
We catch rare glimpses of it
like hungry rabbits listening while eating.
Seems we need luck every now and then.

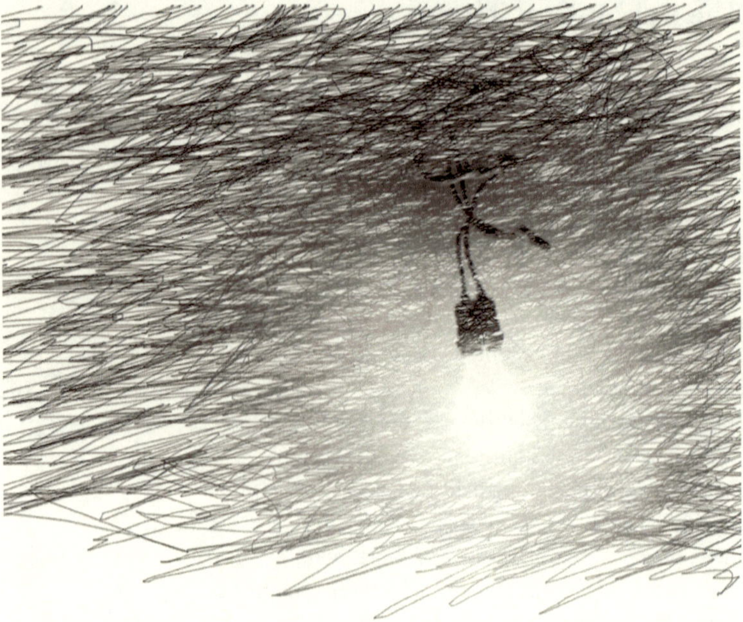

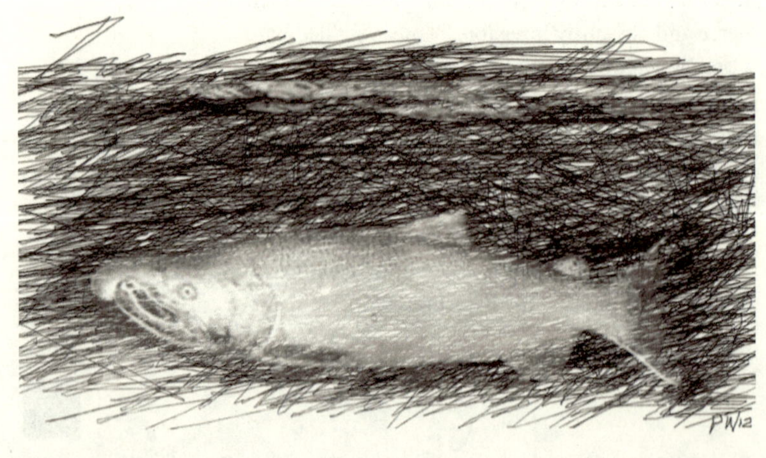
PW12

The Sentence

It was a hit and run strike from out of the peripheral
that occurred so fast, I blinked, thinking of shattered glass.
My other response was also automatic.
Muscle and nerve, with the fast jerk and then swerve of the car.
Didn't work, and the blurred bird was lashed by my whipping antenna.
I saw it bounce once on the shoulder, feathers puffed loose in the mirror,
thinking maybe if I hadn't swerved it would have made it.
Couldn't help it - I swore.
I do this whenever I see dead animals lying there in loose gravel.
Makes me think we're all part of a giant killing apparatus.
None of us are exempt you know.
And for what? Go ahead, ask yourself that.

The dead fawn, still spotted, young, had flies all over it
and the smell is what you first noticed before you even saw it.
Must have laid there for a long time.
It chastised those of us who drove by at fifty or sixty with thin skins.
We thought about it.
Now its family does whatever it does with loss. Sorrow?
I think so.

When I turn on lights I see the silver flashing in waves.
They thrash about powerfully, desperately trying to get past
the dam in their gene's way.
They can't help it. They're driven.
They've been driven for thousands of years.
We're youngsters in comparison and don't know any better.
Don't even wonder about the running water producing that electric light.

I'm at a loss with these thoughts.
Those dead were here and now there's only the empty space they occupied.
It's nothing, yet it's something.
When I drove by yesterday, the bird wasn't there.
The fawn is gone now too. Only a dark spot of dried blood left.
And they say salmon are disappearing. Going extinct.
In my house the light is bright as I write these sentences.
Can't stand the dark.
It's then that it feels like the house is holding me in,
its silence all around me.

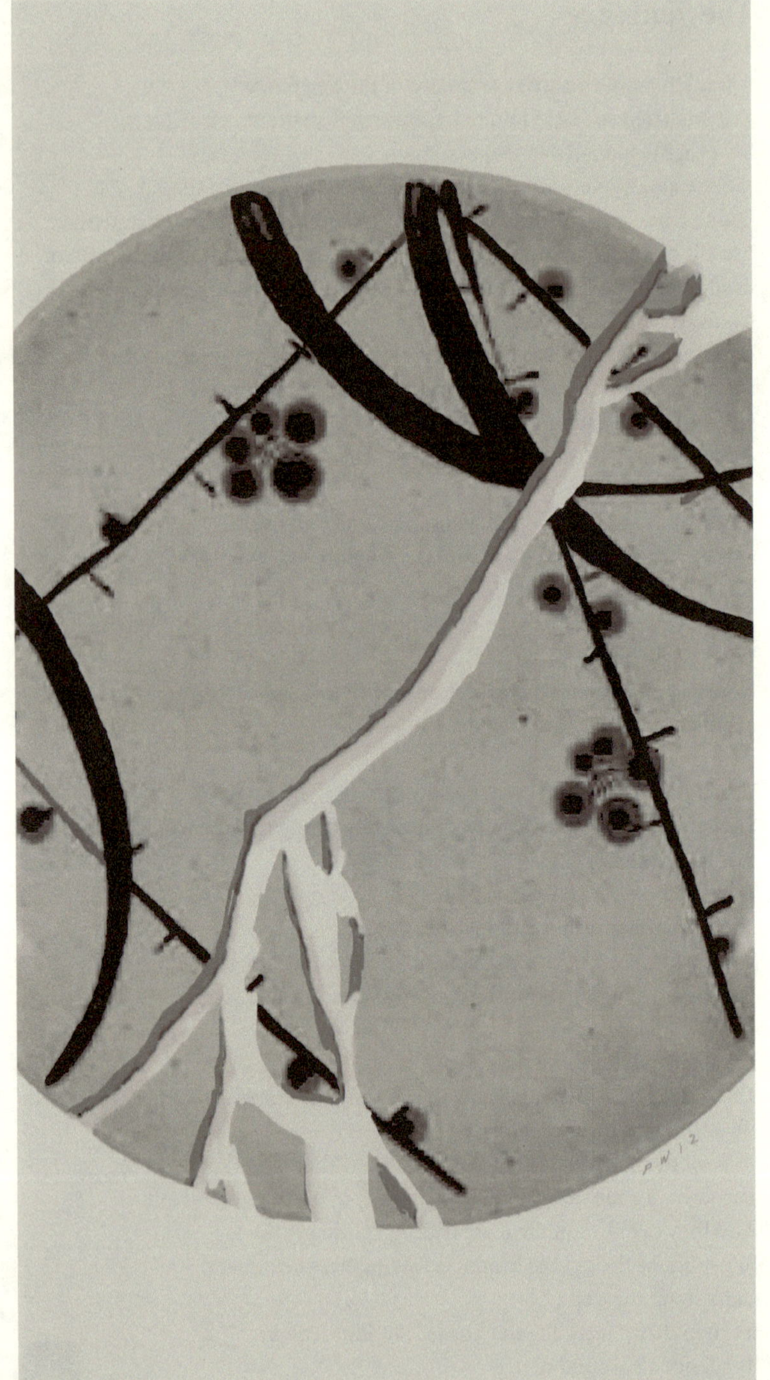
PW12

Kiss Good-bye

This old cheap plate has seen a lot of life.
Chipped and cracked and probably thrown like a missile.
Someone's ex-wife, leaving, probably said, Here. You need a plate.
Hand painted Japanese plum blossoms could take root,
witness to so much life; so much dirt.
Dropped at the thrift store,
a friend, Sam, bought it and gave it to me.
Now it has just died in my sink from wear and tear;
broke apart in slow motion after slipping through my fingers.
The plum blossom branch busted. Flew away. Cut out.
I wonder where Sam is now.
Our relationship severed when he tried to take advantage of me.
A come down.
A black man who loved jazz, women and pot.
On that plate he'd break the stems and loose seeds from the bud
and plunge out of his depth.
Don't know where he went. Disappeared into thin air.
Could be in China for all I know.

On the radio a broadcaster is talking about a black potter -
a slave man - who wrote poetry on all his ceramic wares.
Lived through the Civil War, dying of old age.
Everybody talking about how his pots have been lost to us till now.
They say an old friend is found again.
Memory repaired, won't fall into oblivion.

This Painting

I'm writing this thinking it'll be easy;
something I can get in and out of without too much sweat.
I need this because I'm afraid this painting I should be working on
won't have anything to say when the sun slides down.
Maybe it won't catch hold of anything.
So fear and hesitation made me write this and it flowed out
easy as words being lifted from some dark well.

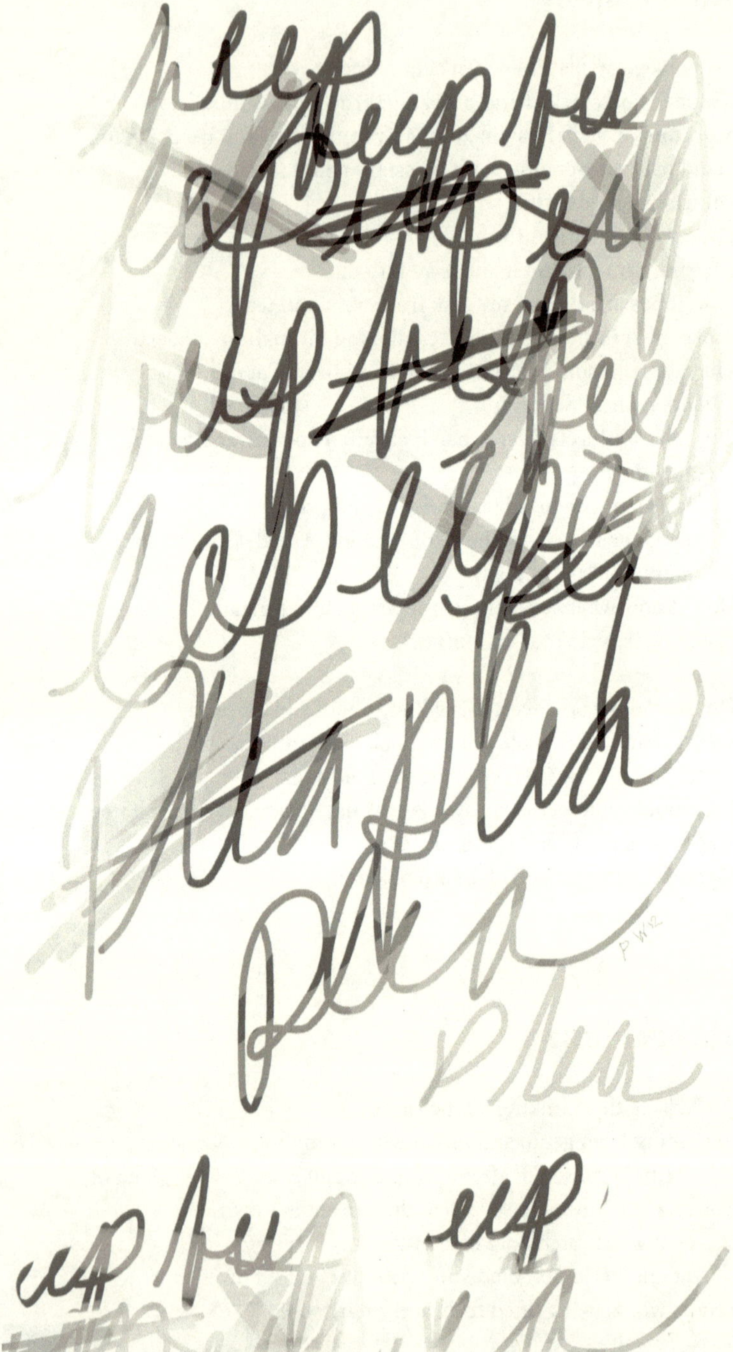

PWR

I Believe in Signs

The coolness of the morning air belies the heat to come.
I round the bumper, moving to the driver's side,
wading through weeds and flowers.
Opening the door, I put my things in the back seat.
The automatic beep, beep, beep tells me the door is open.
It gets to me, hurrying me against myself, insistent.
Off to the side in the tall grass another sound mimics,
but with higher pitch - eep, eep, eep, drawing my eyes down.
At first nothing. Then I see the winding and the coiling,
following the limbless smooth body to its snake head,
mouth gripping a small gray mouse, held by the curved fangs.
Mucus covers its fur and I see it looking up at me
with one eye that can still see out of the snake's mouth.
Its eep, eep, eep is as unending as the car door warning beeps.
Distracting, fear is wrapped in its double vowel stressed plea.
Pangs of remorse shoot through me. They gnaw away at me.
My compassion is strained, hearing this fear; tasting it.
I try telling myself I'm just incarnating it, to relieve anxiety,
but dread builds, striking me at every repeated bleat of panic.
Then pity replaces this. Hesitantly, I know I won't do anything.
I've somehow decided not to interrupt. It's nature.
The mouse's final act fills the snake's need. I'm audience.
I quickly jump in, closing door, and start the car's engine.
Tires dig out, spitting gravel as I attempt to rid the eep, eep sound.
Want to hear other sounds instead; maybe song of highway.
But humming tires won't let me kill its memory.
I still hear its high tone; its soulful - please, please, please.
The heated blacktop wavers in and out ahead of me
as I keep a sharp eye peeled on opposing traffic.

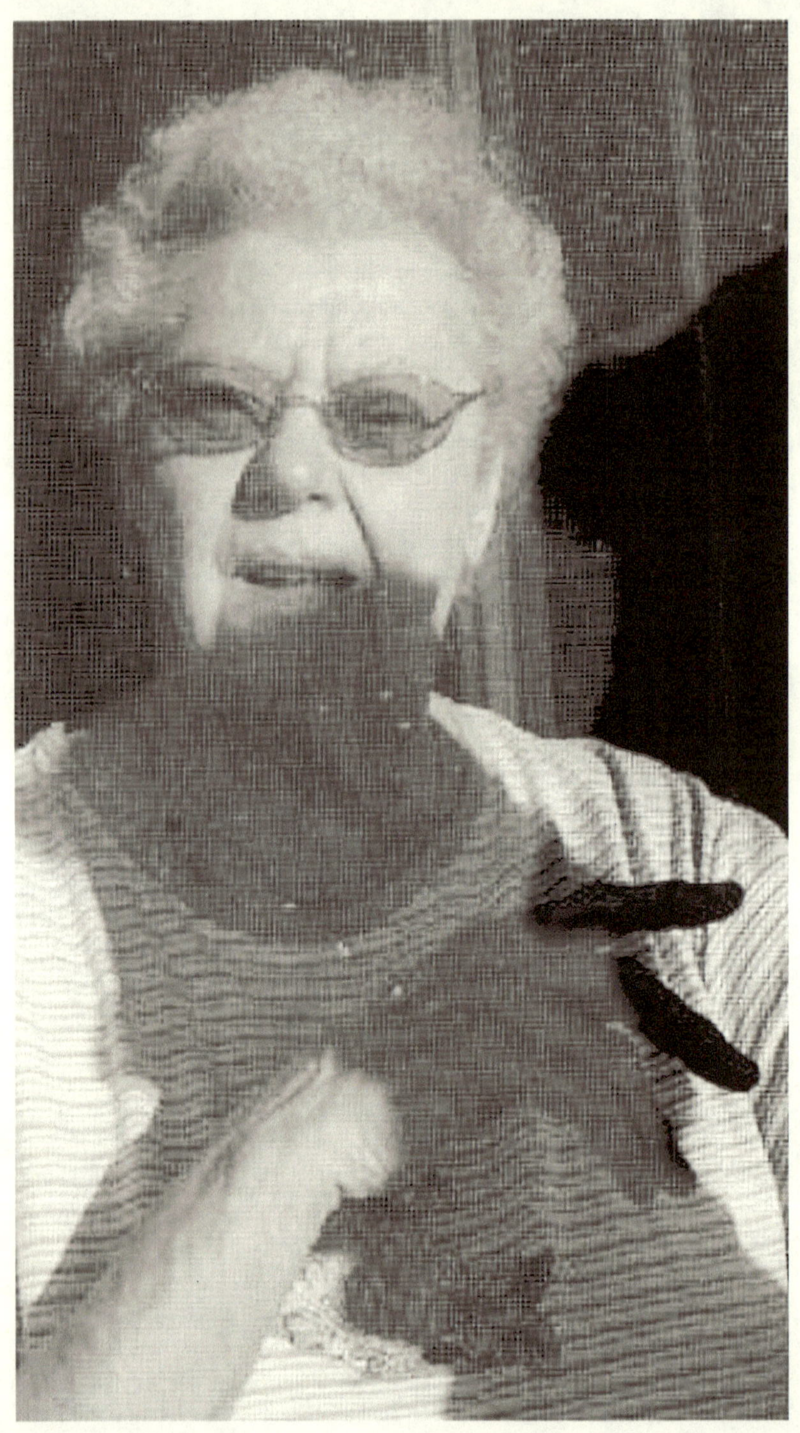

Tied To

For Adele

In a straight line from car door to house door
I follow your daughter into your home,
not knowing and with a little trepidation,
as if I'm a trespasser trespassing a certain line;
the family ties that bind.
A timeless scene, you make it special
with your warm ease: "gracious," I told Judith.
Easygoing, you say, "Well, you're in good shape,"
and I know your charm instantly
and become unknotted as if you've thrown me a lifeline.
Smiling with you we breathe free and easy,
words embracing, no strings attached,
while Judith tries balancing your bank account -
a high wire walk into thinner air.
Afterwards we inspect stairs to the basement
where you thread your way down into the dark
by hanging to a rope we talk about remaking
as a two-by-four, something that can be easily grasped.
I hang indoor plant, watered, dripping,
then replace outdoor hose that leaks coiled
like a snake waiting for the night bugs attracted by light.
Meanwhile, Judith weeds the flowers,
cleaning their beds for them to wake from,
welcoming them like roses in May.
As we turn, you present us with camera
attempting to cage and train the view
into memories to look at tomorrow.
Three shots it takes to capture:
first, me and Jude; second, you and Jude; then, you and me;
camera passed at all the smiles in the line of sight.
We leave too soon.
I say, "Good bye Adele. Nice meeting you Adele,"
and you lean forward waiting to be kissed -
so natural to kiss, to say good bye to;
your grace and beauty drawing an elegant line
of warm human sympathy.
Riding back, my mind reaches out, taking kindly to you, at ease.
At ease all the way to the end of the line, and beyond.

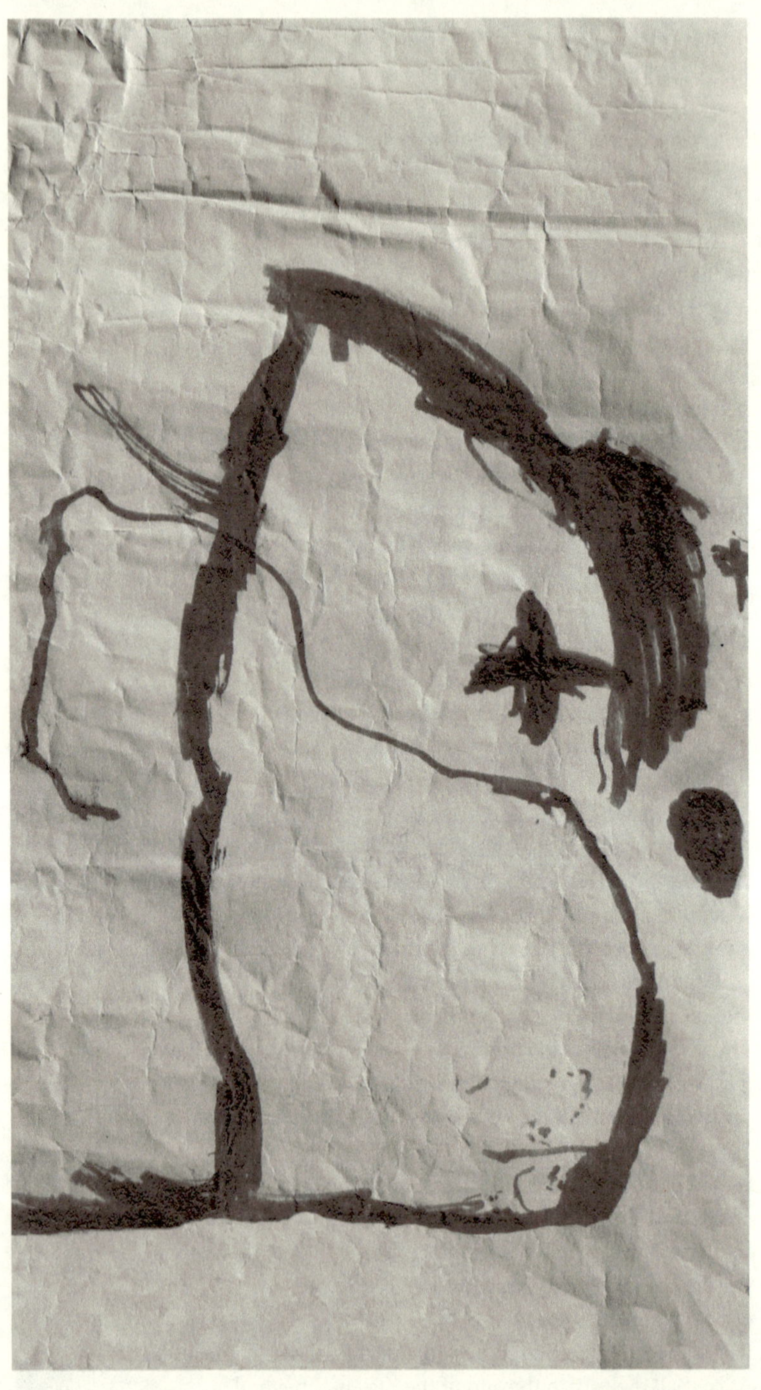

Found Drawing

Not Only Pebble on Beach

Beach this morning is a whirl of activity, but for all that, I keep walking.
Take everything in stride as I do every morning out here on the cove.
Dogs see little, if any of this, lost to their own world,
concerned with smelling, looking under driftwood and trotting down
to cool themselves in that water not far from the Pacific.
They know I keep a steady pace and try to make the most of each walk.
Sun's bright in clear bird's-egg-blue sky but clouds roll in fast off the Strait.
See rain sheets slant down and gray view of distant Olympic Mountains.
With the sunlight in front of me I like to look for agates.
Look for where light passes through them, coloring surrounding sand.It's
semi-precious light I look for, not the rocks themselves.
Take in all this. Stunning. Crowds out other thoughts for a bit. Just a bit.
Then they wash back in like the tide. Impossible to hold them back.
All kinds of things surface. Sometimes memories.

The one this morning, bittersweet, thinking back to when I was six.
Missing the school bus, the willow switch on my calves hurt my feelings.
Defiant, I hid in the woods. I wasn't going to walk, as Dad insisted.
He figured he'd pick me up along the way. First, wanted to mollify me.
Driving all the way to the school, he didn't find me.
Got scared. Called sheriff. Had a search party.
I timed it to walk into the farm after the bus passed my hiding spot.
Had it all figured out. Instead, sheriff read me the riot act.
Wanted to know what I'd eaten. "Grass!", I said.

Funny how that surfaced, unexpected. For a minute or two I'm lost to it.
Stooping, seeing the amber light passing through stone,
I realize what I've trampled on all these years.
In rising up to my father that time, I'd hardened myself to his authority.
Freed myself. Even now I stiffen a bit to his advice,
like willow must stiffen, when hitting other limbs.

These are pacific thoughts this morning, with the dogs in the distance
and salt water lapping the shore without an undertow.
Further on I stumble onto a capped bottle, paper message rolled inside.
With the excitement of discovery, I open and pull out a child's drawing.
Looks like the kid could be about six. No kidding. Six.
Something or other must be going on here.

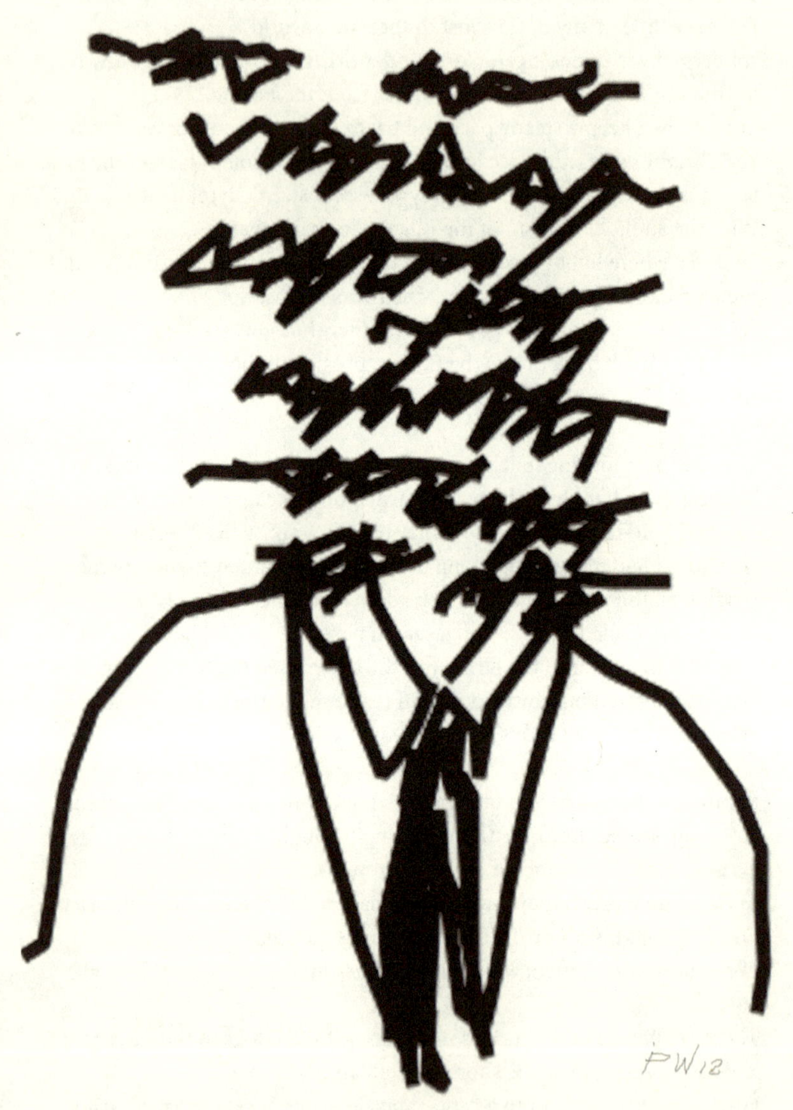
PW12

We Gather Here Today

12:21am, "Started with hitting each other with bats and one was hit
in face with flashlight, trying to make 'em see the light," said the officer.
2:09am, Neighbor reports loud hot tub party: "They'll be in hot water".
3:43am, Pleasant View resident reported hiding from landlord who arrives
unannounced and starts screaming at her for no reason what so ever.
5:06am, Rural man reports death threat by sister-in-law.
6:03am, City man assaulted by brother-in-law.
9:17am, Boy of eleven goes out of control. Punches holes in unfinished
drywalled bathroom. Mother can't handle, "...cause I'm beside myself."
10:26am, Pawn shop employee tells of young boy wanting to buy rifle.
11:03am, Woman overhears young male student threatening
to shoot her only pre-teen daughter. No weapon displayed.
11:35am, Person in red Toyota reportedly threw gum wrapper out window
on Highway 20. Deputy totally unable to locate the errant litterer.
12:34pm, Stolen: Toolbox, Ford 250 pickup, a futon, safe with fire alarm,
a flute and clarinet. Pieced together that thief used tools for truck
to haul mattress to absorb shock of blown safe causing alarm
which scares him off, grabbing horns on way out.
12:45pm, Adventure Electronic Alarms is burglarized again.
1:26pm, A Reservation Road resident reports cane stolen.
1:45pm, Woman reports neighbor below threatens her
by thumping on the ceiling with something pointed.
2:02pm, Transit employee reports someone in medium sized boat
trying to run over a large gray whale in the small end of Cove.
2:21pm, Ill resident requests officer get rid of pig fetus
from her home that she thinks is really making her sick.
3:18pm, Girl bears witness that bus driver pushed her down.
4:45pm, Highway 20 Restaurant spreads rumor chef purloining food.
He goes crazy, makes threats and is verbally abusive. Runs out.
7:47pm, S.W. Third Ave. resident alludes that car is "egged."
8:56pm, Eggs thrown at passersby on S.E. Pioneer.
9:47pm, At Harvest Drive, falling can of beans dents car hood.
10:38pm, Woman throws money at late shopping Walmart customers.
"Those damn floodlights are too much," she shrieks.
11:01pm, Woman harassing bouncers at male strip joint off Buck Road.
11:30pm, 80 year old woman's unattended death at 1754 Shady Lane.
"She was a real loner," said the attending officer.

For richer or poorer, in sickness and in health.

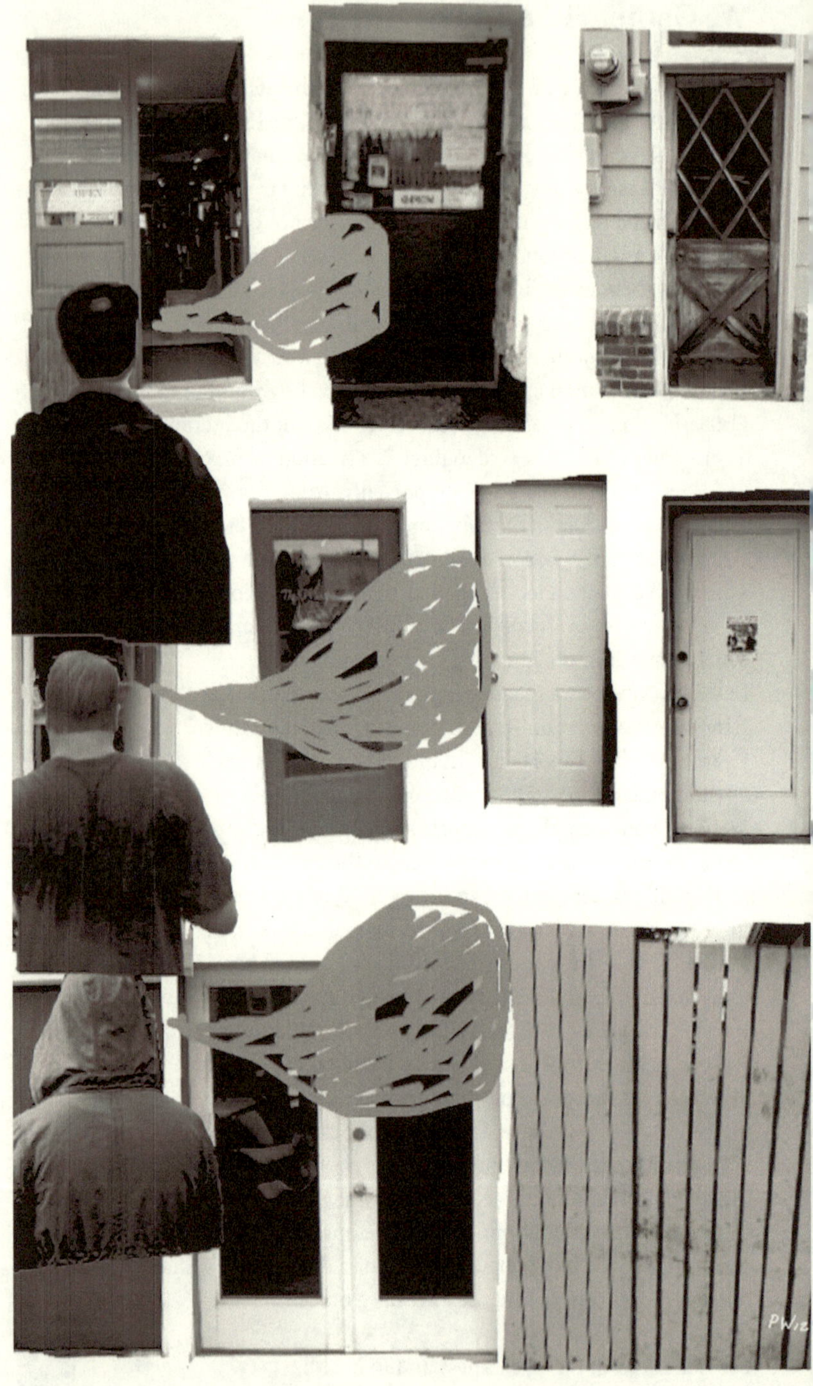

Talk is Cheap

Taxed while
talking in circles,
the man of few words
had his words
taken right out of his mouth.

Deductions

I hear the cats hissing and whining
but can't see them.
Can only imagine
their cold wet matted fur flying.
Eeeow! Cat fight.
This easily sidetracks me. I whine too.
I don't want to do my taxes.
I don't want to digress into last year.
Don't want circling memories arching back.
Eeeow! Give me a break.
Now look!
Halfway through the checkbook
I've landed on it before realizing it was there.
I'm catapulted into the pain and tears of July.
She's dead!
There I am, my sobs clawing at darkness,
not wanting any diversions
from my good hairy roll in grief.
Something about the pain of this
comforts my heart; comforts its torn-apartness.
I recognize it as being human.
That's what it was you know.
I saw that I had it, after all.
Tastes bitter but sweet and I wanted it to myself.
Wanted to cage it so I could savor at will.
Pull its fangs. Make it cry "Uncle".
Or is that "Sam"?
Taxing!
Eeeow!

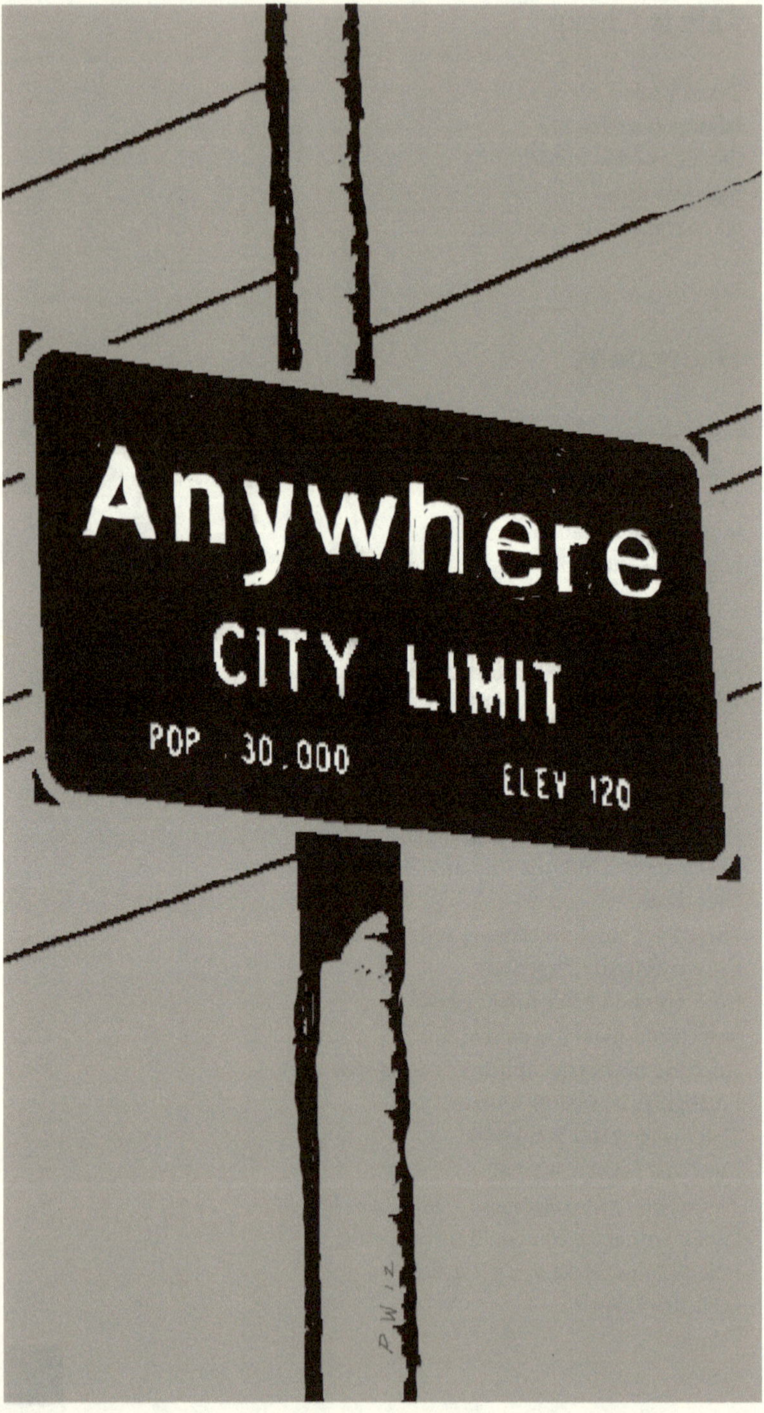

Anywhere
CITY LIMIT
POP 30,000
ELEV 120

Swan Song

I come gliding around the hill.
See brush smoke near Swantown exit.
White and long necked, curving up,
signaling another mass construction.
Can't miss it. Please, no more signals.
Site sign, bulldozer, back hoe, dump
truck trying to hatch new homes.
Moving dirt to strike it rich.
Say good bye vegetation!
I wing it down past the work
on that huge concrete block wall
and hope they mural it, but now
a small sign nesting crooked says,
Coming Soon-Albertsons Food & Drug.
Not very pretty. All this laboring
while businesses are closing.
The talk at Chamber lunches
amounts to wishing for tourist dollars.
They want more feathers in their caps,
but the feathers are flying.
I don't need a truck
to get me down in the dumps.
I'm already there. Anywhere, USA.
Heard Swantown was named
for all the swans who used to be there.
Trumpeters, I think.
Fed on the greenery.
Must of heard our horns as we rode in,
flying in the face of nature
for more food and drugs.

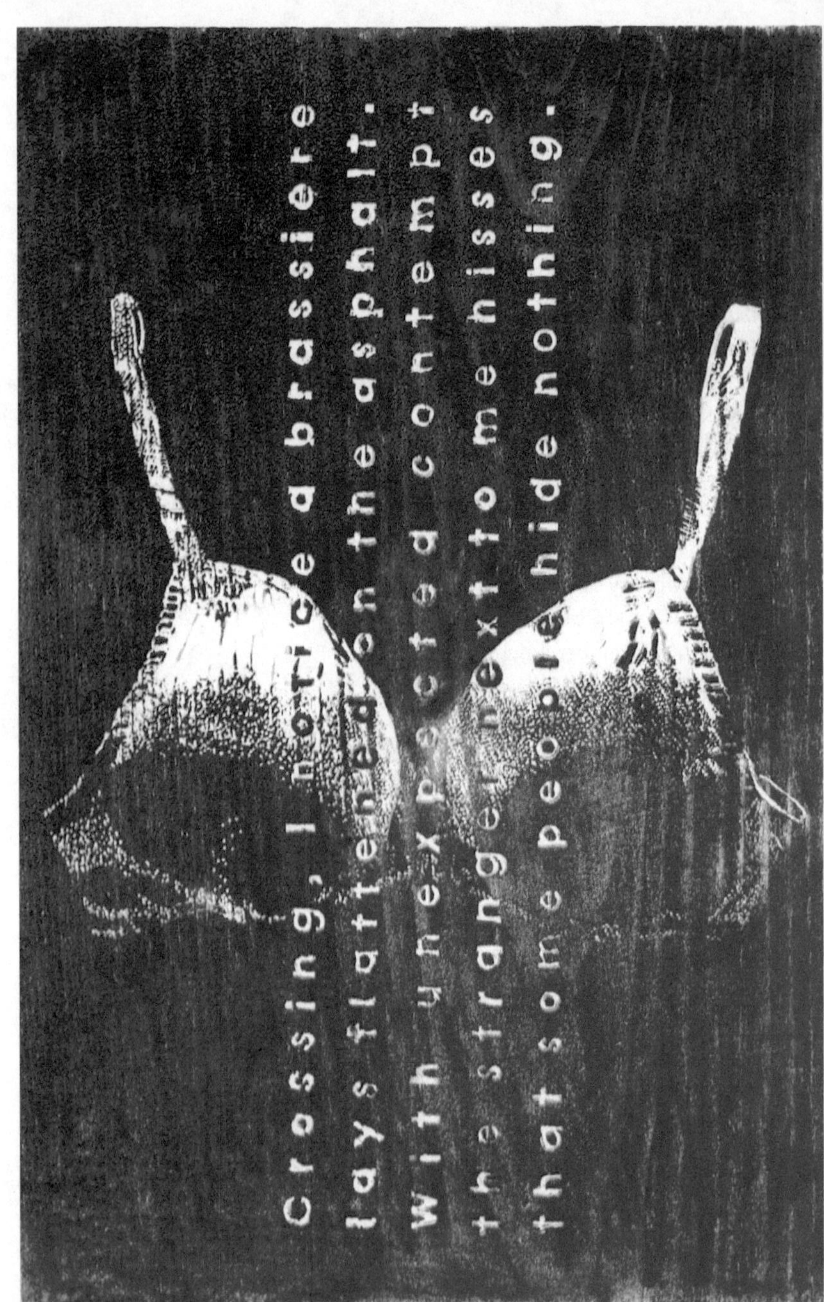

2002 Woodcut Print titled, *Free.*

A Hat Trick Too Much for TV

Found a black beret on the road in front of my house
and it wants to talk, to tell me all the particulars.
Sitting on my kitchen table, yesterday it simply said
it belonged to a drunk who drove between taverns,
first getting thrown out of one and then another.
Drinking and thus not working, he was so poor
he sold his hair to a doll restorer and without hair
the beret was too large, falling off in the headwind
on the way to the next bar, just before the collision.
Jailed on a DWI, cellmates thought he was hairless
and couldn't get over the coincidence of the eagle
chest tattoo, calling him "Old Baldy" behind his back.

Today it said that it had belonged to a famous actress
who, while driving, talked with her agent on a phone,
not noticing the drunk round the bend prior to crash.
Her car was totaled, but what really pissed her off was
finding out the promised part went to someone else.
Throwing beret down, she had a fit, dancing in ditch,
until they strapped her down for the trip to the asylum.

Tomorrow this same beret will probably tell me it was
on the actress when the drunk, who was concerned,
rescued her from burning car, as she melted with desire
into his arms in hot surrender, which aroused him
and as he fumbled to put one of his hands under her bra,
she arched forward to aid him and didn't feel the cap
fall away when his other hand began to move downward.

I listen to all this while staring at it resting on the table,
and honestly wonder about the reminder of its history.
I know I've been carried away by my own imagination
but it's fun to get caught up in dreams and play in them.
They settle on me like dust flakes resting on a TV screen
and it becomes second nature to invent these soap operas
while tuning in a channel to talk through a hat to myself.

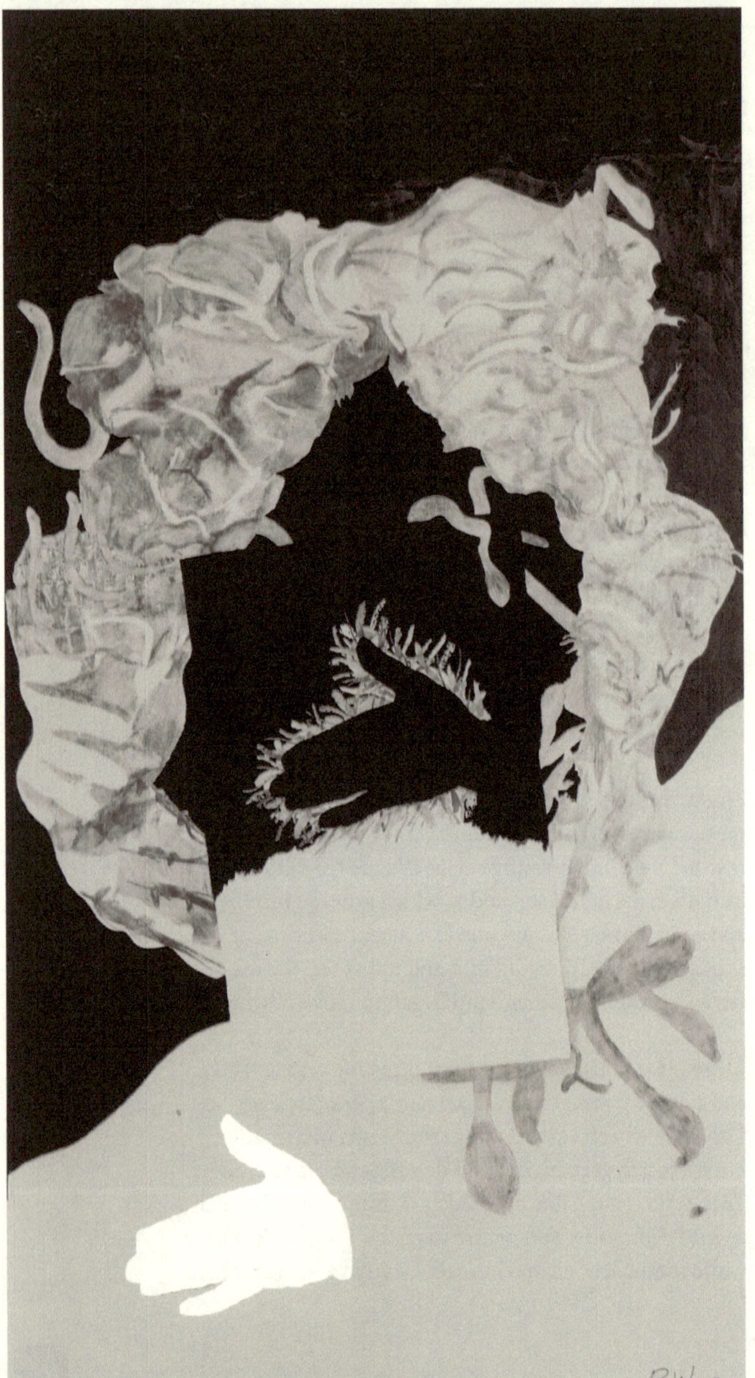
PW'12

Hogging the Light

Crying as I sensed its squealing dread,
Father curses while Mother frets
and tongues of fire lick the big black pot.
We drag it across dirty ground
by lasso to the Lincoln car bumper,
not unlike memory hidden then found.
Occassionally this springs to life
as smoke coils before the flame.
Tied to it like a bristled frozen hunter
kneeling before embers,
it roots in my brain around and around
flickering in and out.
Childhood appears from darkness
often flanked in unwanted luminosity
and at night I reach to turn it off
but the pigheaded sun returns unhailed.

The Presence of Home

The Sound

It's all around you.
You see the water everywhere.
It surrounds you.

And sometimes you become a kid again.
The salt in the air takes you there.
You skip stones on its waves.
You look for light piercing its agates.

And those close to you ask,
Can you spread my ashes in it?
Cementing itself, it's home to you.

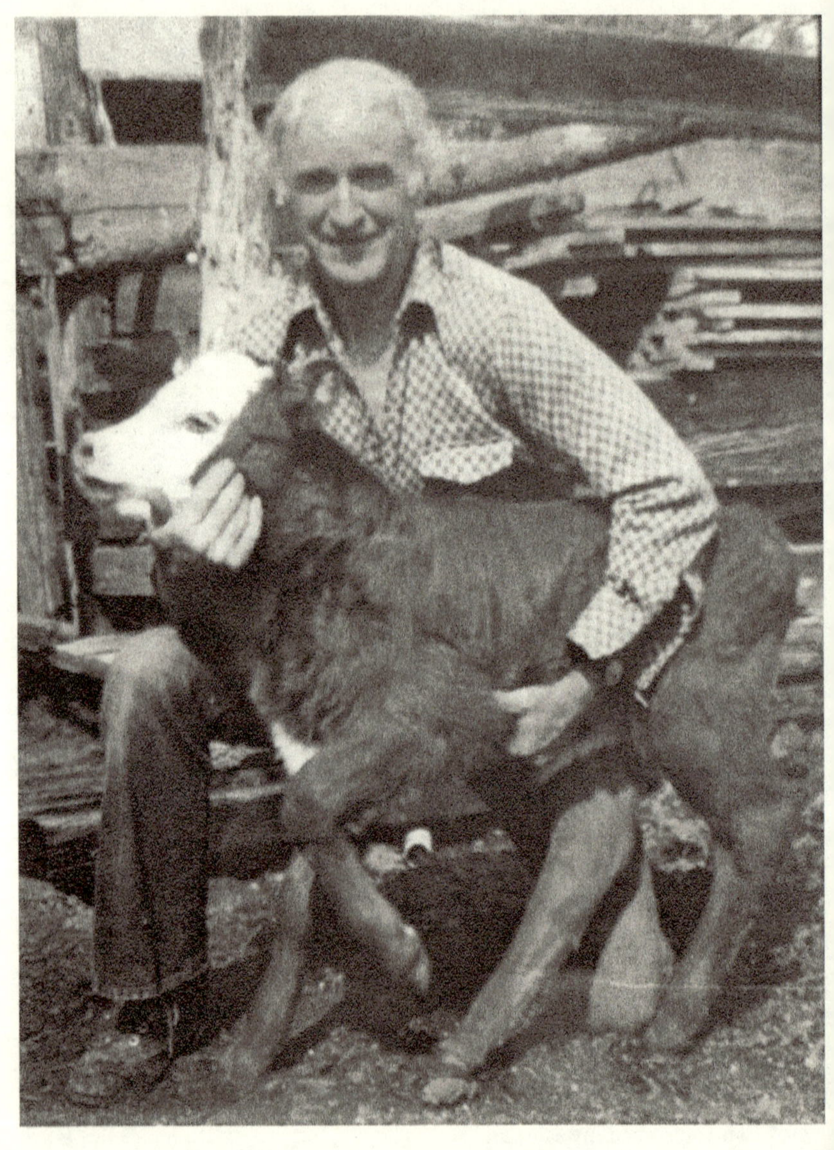

What Is Not Written

For my Father

The poems I did not write you
are wet with tears, like ink,
as if written just now.
We know they surfaced off and on
through time, unpredictable,
taking turns like a group of whales
sounding out the depth.

Beyond Measure

For my Father

We talk with our eyes locked on each other's
the way you taught me to as a boy,
showing, that we take each other seriously.

My eyes film. I take this to heart.
I know I'll talk to you like this for years to come,
until light disappears from my eyes too.

I'll talk eye to eye to you about your love,
over and over thanking you,
but diminished, unable to pay back a memory.

Flick

As a kid, pretending to be Roy Rogers, each bang of my B-B gun rang true.
Faith in this role made the impossible so believable that one day
when I hit a robin, its thud on the ground matched my heart.
I never forgot it dying, warm to my hand,
feathers fluttering against a gathering wind.
Its death was not sweet, not some revenge on bad guys,
and with good and bad wavering and disappearing like a mirage,
I had my first taste of remorse.
This memory is a feature that plays often,
trailing across my lit up screen inside.

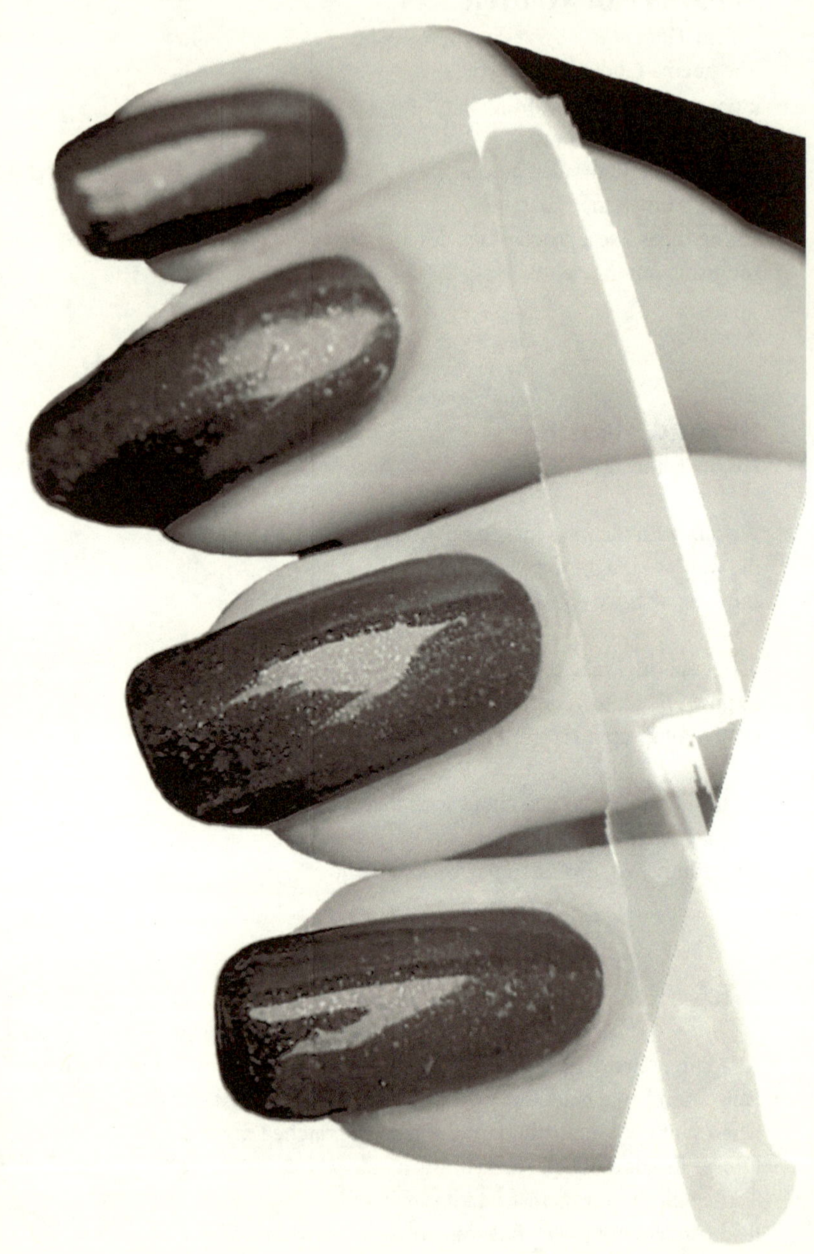

PW 12

Brought to You By

It's raining in the dark.
They can hear it, sitting at the table watching who cares what.
Just watching the little Sony black and white
perched there across from them on the thick stack of bills.
It screeches at them shrilly now and then.
Sometimes there's fake canned laughter, a twittering of sorts.
And in between, the rain on the roof.
They smoke a lot. He drinks.
All it does is make for unease. A tensing.

It's a real question as to who started it.
Maybe it just boiled to the surface on its own
after so much disappointment and leanness.
Debt has hung over them for too long.
A swinging sword, it's about to cut off their civility.
Any small thing can send them over the edge
because of the sheer accumulation.

Breaking first, she turns in her chair,
her wrath pushing restraint out of the way.
Yelling incoherently, she whacks away at his chest,
pelting him with her rage, lips curved, teeth clenched.
It's a real beating. It drowns out the rain; the TV.
He stands this as long as he can and then reaches out,
grabbing her fists midair, attempting to deny her.
Their eyes meet and the anger is disarming; wilting.
Their dogs have withdrawn into opposite corners, shaken.
She stands and wrings her wrists free, shouting,
You son of a bitch. You no good bastard.
He lays his eyes on her, sneering,
the misshapen smile meant as scorn; contempt.
He sees knives and daggers exit her pupils.
She comes at him again with her fingers and nails curved.
They rake across him leaving blood on his cheek.
He jumps up and pushes her away, backward,
and she trips over a chair, falling to the unfinished floor.

On the TV, a woman in a sweet voice
talks about how Revlon is the best at drying;

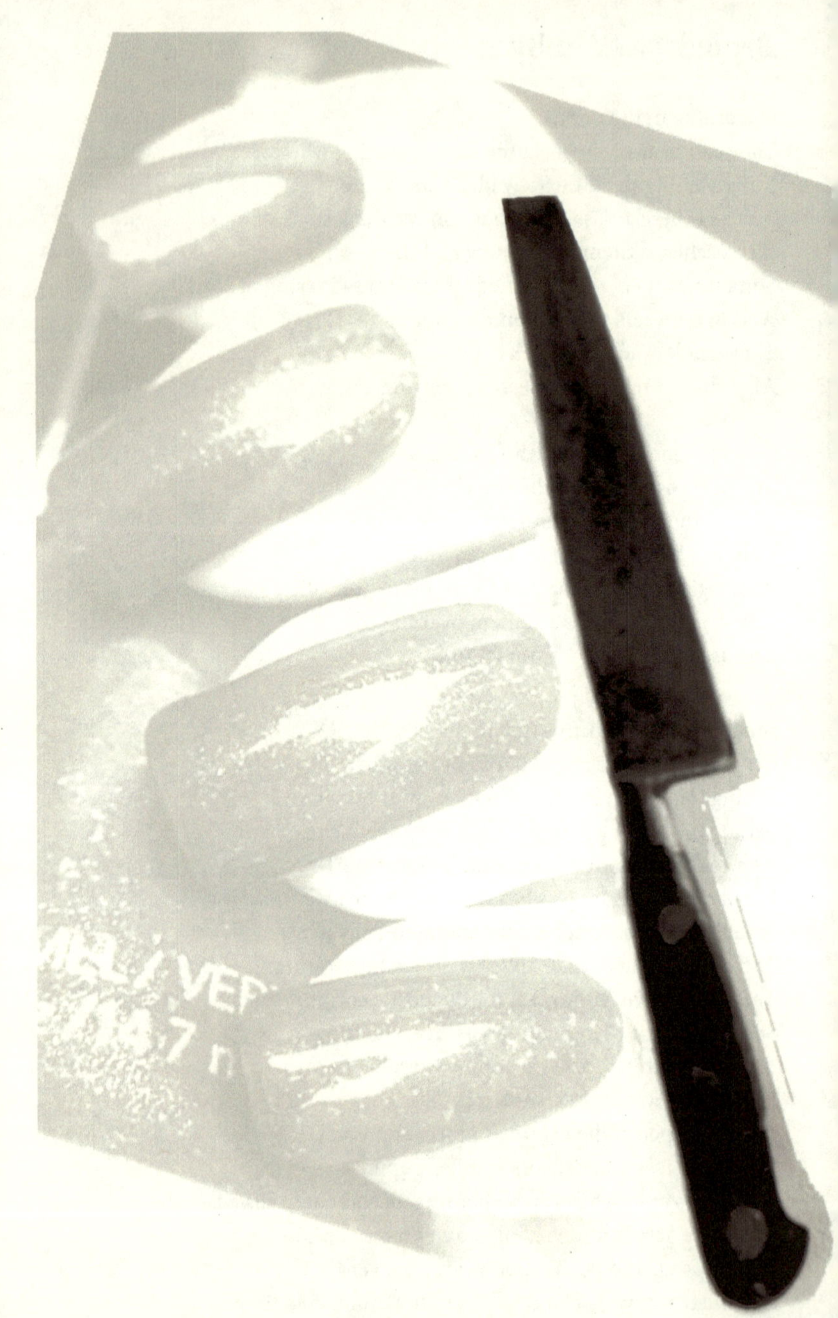

PW12

how their speed dry nail color will set you free
in ninety seconds - with money back guarantee.
He sits back down, not hearing this,
mind seething, unable to concentrate.
He pretends unconcern. Pretends to watch the Sony.
Doesn't see or hear it, but pretends to.
Following ad wants him to buy Tic Tac.
Something about Friendly Breath is in the Air.
He sees and hears only her, in his peripheral senses.
She's dragging herself up slow like.
The Sony says, Welcome to Jeopardy!
Audience claps as she walks into the kitchen deliberately.
Then something about, Famous Couples for 200,
and, By the People Who Make Healthy Choice.

The butcher knife flies past him parting the dense close air.
People are clapping again.
It hits the rough floor, blade first, tip snapping off.
Now there's crying. And very heavy rain.
The bills just sit there.

Fresh

I tilled all day to plant poppies.
Spring has come - I want a fresh start.
Next I rearrange my entire house
then wake with a stiff neck.
It hurts - have to turn my whole body to see around me.
The smell of fresh ground coffee seems to help.
Outside the turned soil is alive
with robins hunting fleshy worms.
In the sky is a rainbow and below,
the deep blue water of the cove sparkles with promise.
The sun comes through the clean glass easier now.
Glancing up from the floor, it hits me in the face,
and for a moment I forget the pain
and the fact that hard work
tires me more than it used to.
Sometimes it feels like I'm just a prisoner of myself
living too fast, dying too slow.

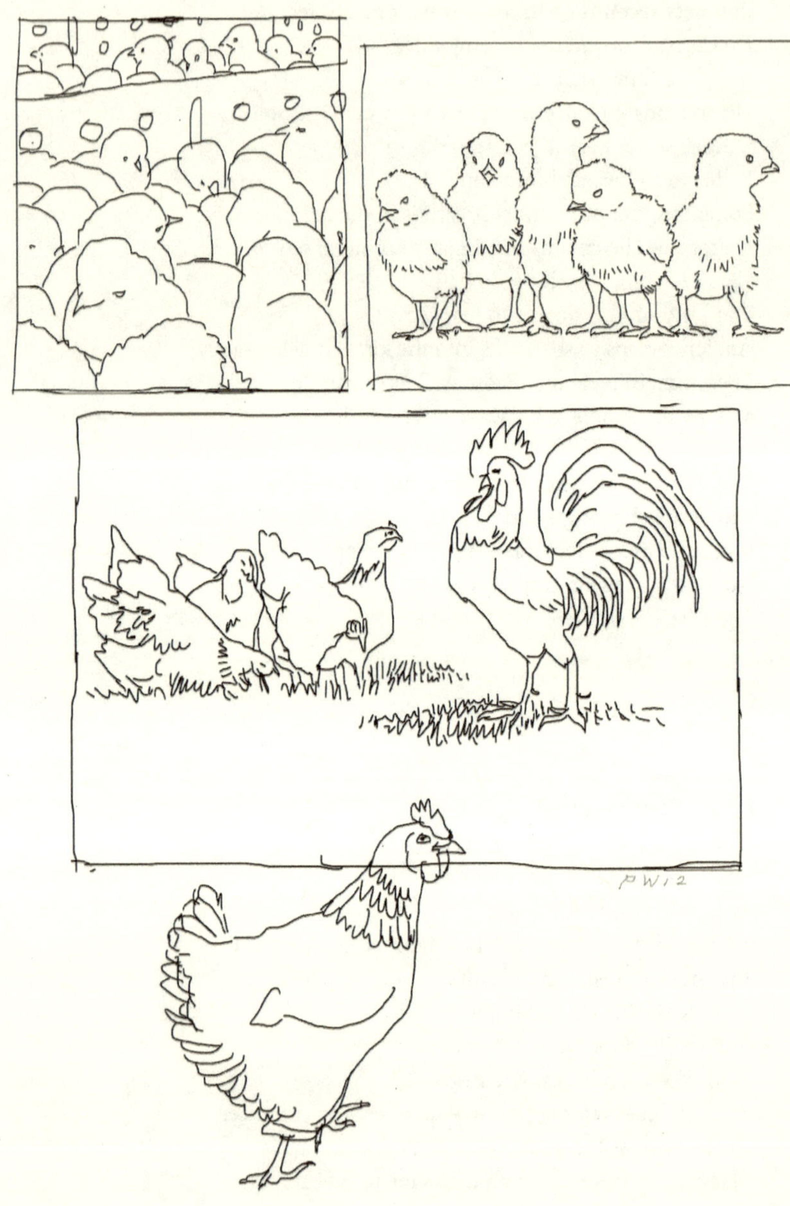
PW12

Chicken Feed

For the life of me I can't remember his name.
It's hiding on the tip of my tongue.
It's right there but I can't reach it.
I think it was Whitey.
But that's probably only because he was blond...
or was it red hair,
and he was a big man and blue eyed - fair.
Dad liked him, I could tell.
They talked a lot whenever he came with another batch
of those little yellow baby chicks
that chirped away under cover,
locked in that perforated cardboard box they came in.

And those chicks were cute. At first.
So cute you couldn't keep your hands away from them.
But then they'd grow
and then I'd be out there sweating, collecting their eggs.
That was my job.
I'd "shoo" the laying hens away from their nests
and real quick, grab any eggs that lay there.
Felt like I was stealing them
in the quiet of six A.M. mornings before grade school.
I wondered if I left them,
left them to be kept warm by the hens,
whether they'd turn into chicks too.

And I learned to drink coffee then,
holding the steaming cup in both hands
and bringing it to my lips
to warm me on those early cold mornings
before going out there and facing
those chickens and their eggs again.
Sometimes running late and in a hurry to catch the school bus,
I'd accidentally drop one and see its white shell
crack open at my feet.
Its contents, its white and its yellow yoke,
would run out onto the sawdust bedding
and I'd feel terrible - a criminal.
Felt like those hens, all of them, *(Continued on next page.)*

WANTED

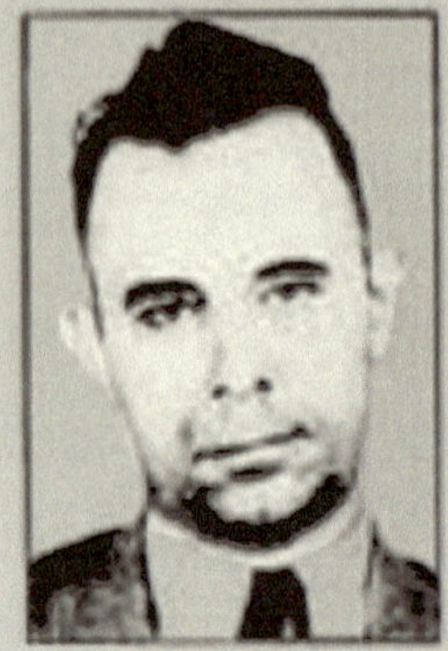

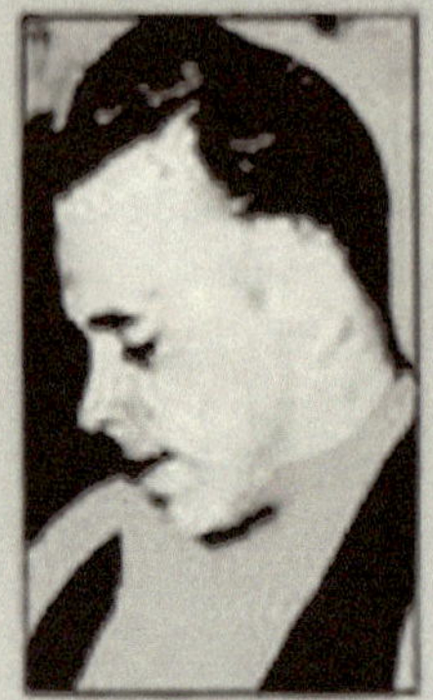

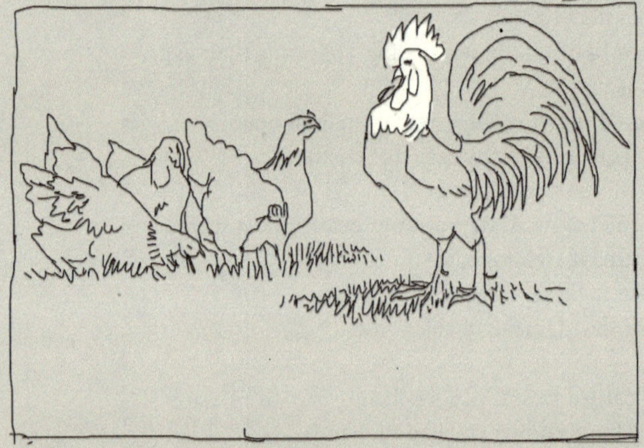

On June 23, 1934, HOMER S. CUMMINGS, Attorney General of the United States, under the authority vested in him by an Act of Congress approved June 6, 1934, offered a reward of

$10,000.00

for the capture of John Herbert Dillinger or a reward of

$5,000.00

for information leading to the arrest of John Herbert Dillinger.

CHICKEN FEED

would stop pecking or doing whatever they were doing,
and just stare at me.

Anyway, when they were chicks, they were cute
and I'd pet their soft innocent feathers
while Dad and Whitey talked away.
Absorbed, I never really listened to their conversations.
They talked about things I wasn't interested in.
Talked a lot about money and trying to scratch out a living.
Didn't know it then, but later, don't exactly know when,
Dad told me Whitey used to rob banks.
He was an expert at cracking safes.
During the Depression, his services were in demand.
He'd sit there quiet, twirling those tumblers in the dark,
listening and feeling for the combination
that'd crack open the door.
When it did, it must have been a real rush,
all that easy money just sitting there, staring at him,
ready for the plucking.

Have to admit, I've dreamed of robbing banks.
Wouldn't like being caged behind bars though,
but in my dreams I never get caught.
In them, it's as easy as stamping my feet
and the bank doors fly open like feathers flying
and dollar bills come floating down out of nowhere.
Just dreams though. That's all. Just dreams.
Whitey actually got caught.
In those times, didn't all criminals get caught?
And I guess he was in the pen for years.
Dad said he'd gotten the tattoo on his forearm while in there.
It was a picture of a cock crowing in front of a bunch of hens.
Never failed to gather in my wandering eyes.
Wish I could remember Whitey's name.
An older man, he seemed happy working for chicken feed.

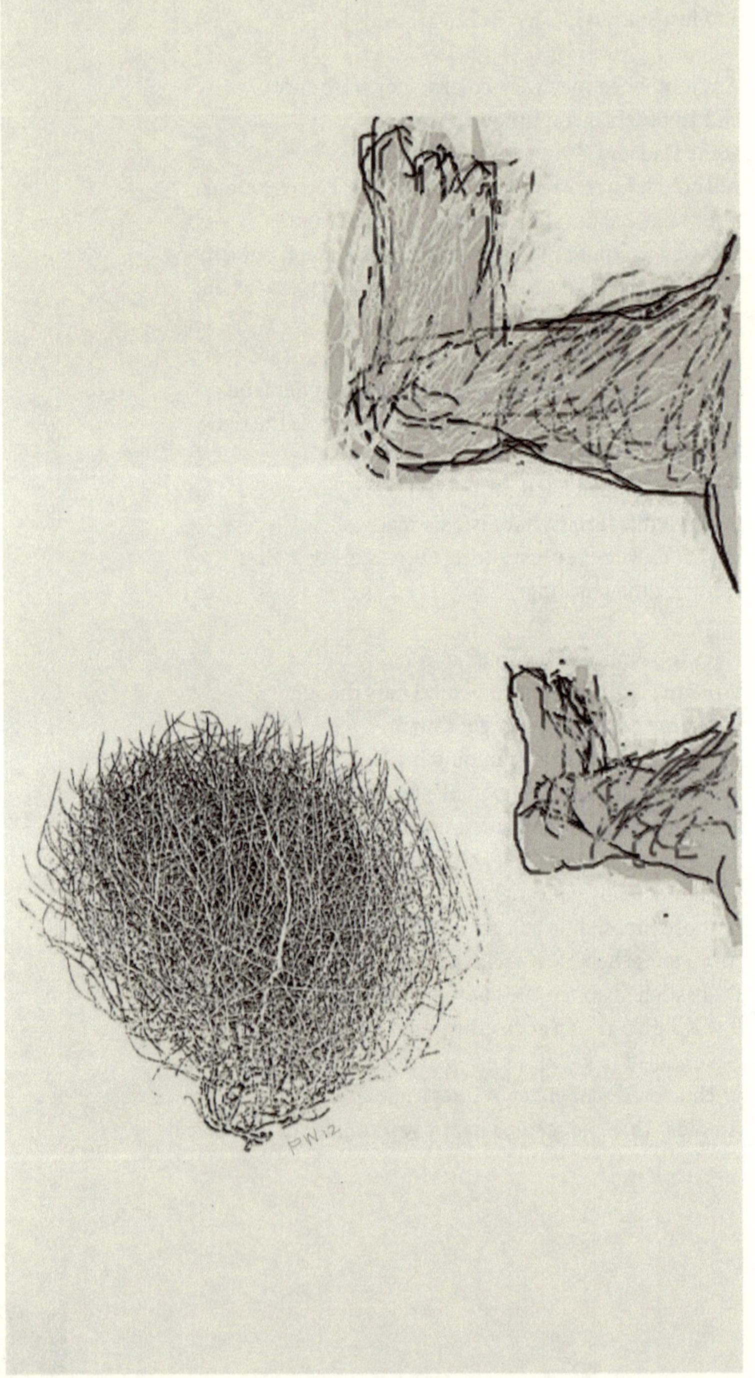
PW12

Unfinished

Two people!
Male and female.
They argue.
Their words move through air,
clashing head on.
The collision forms
blood red bullets.
Teeth clench
like closed white fences.
Divorce hangs
in a heavy field.
Palpable, it drips black.
Considering whether
the number three is irrelevant,
a child is pushed
to the bottom.

The two think
the child will survive.
Things like this pass, they say,
like wind sweeping away dust.
The child will play in it, they say,
because children think things.
Like maybe tumbleweeds are sails
instead of something
that needs to be taken away
and wiped out.
But these people don't know
that this is the child's roots
and children never forget.
Cut off, their souls are ground away
as if they'd been sprayed
by scolding inhalations.

Flying South

Out there on water
two ducks glide down
with their feet raking a thin line
in the silvery blue surface.
Not long from now
you and your best friend
will part clouds
as your metal plane
carries you toward the sun.
Distant from me with the distance
about to grow further,
your invisibility drives me
to slip love into occasional poems.
Most hover on electronic air
so I thought it'd be a send-off gift
for you to actually see one up close.
The curve of my letters
and how I combine them
may stir and move you.
My grade school teachers
worked hard on penmanship
but you know,
they never taught us anything
about the art of losing.
Even though you're going away,
I'll be there
wanting to skim silently over you.

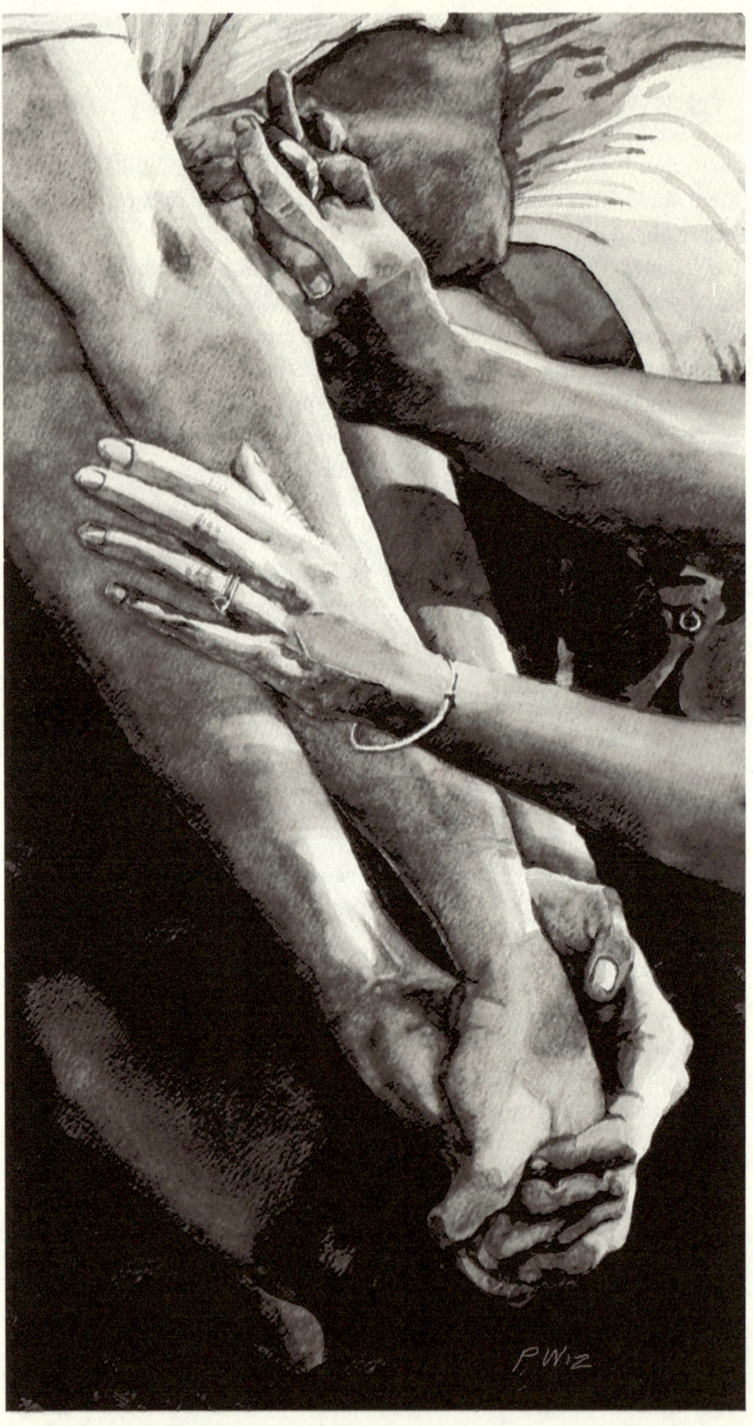
P. Wiz

Praying for a Ship to Sail

Great Time,
immense and encompassing,
weave something
to cover things up.
Oh please warp with your yarns.
Shuttled under your waving web,
we know your great darkness
can comfort, can weft us away.
We need this during certain moments.
Our fingers are interlaced
in prayer before you.
We pray memory of those we lost,
their soft lips under moon's touching desire,
disappears in your shadow;
disappears next to the waves of loneliness.
Keep us from remembering.
Let us go.
Let us go past the looming monument
of commitment by heart.
Oh Great Degrader,
fold us under your waving patterns,
your ocean of the pacific.
We must say good-bye.
Dead people are...it's like...
What's it like?...like a ship.
Let us wave good-bye.
Up and down,
we'll keep them in our own course.
Let the memory of them that rises unbidden
dip into your waves
with the thin needle
of your threading sun.

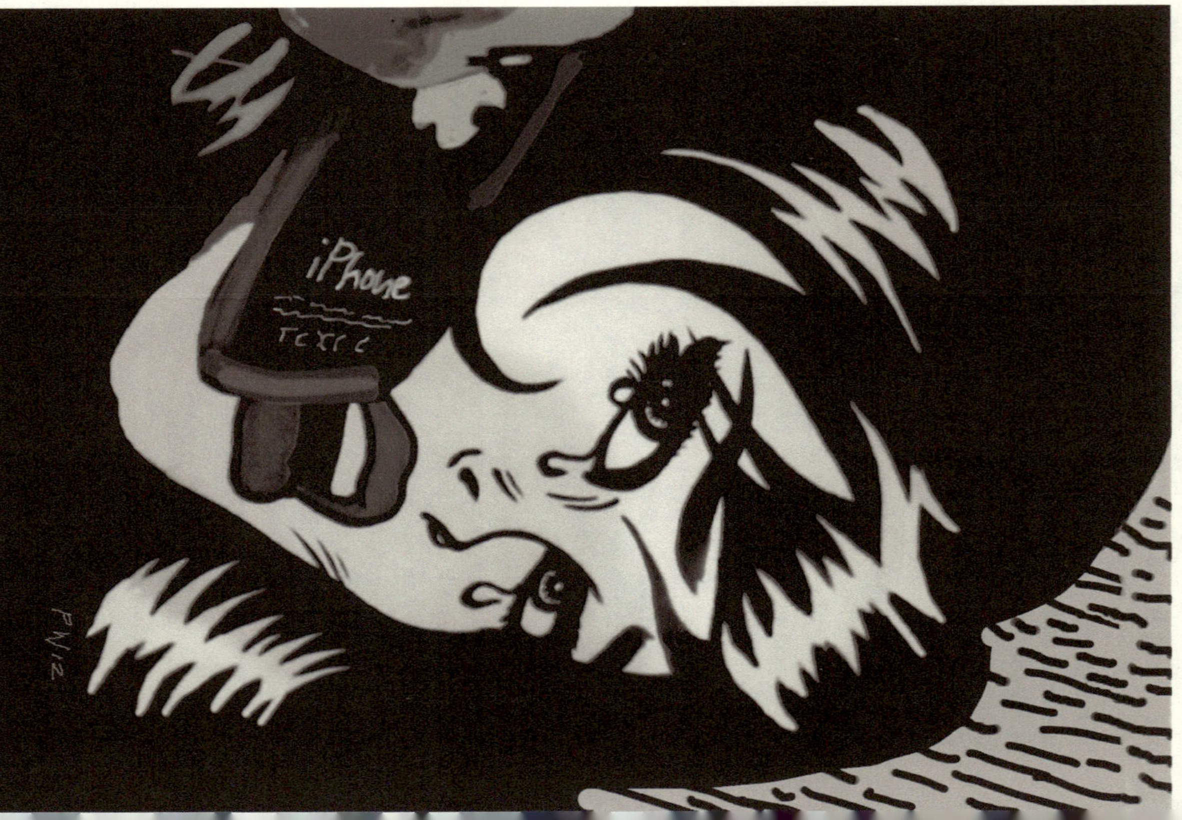
iPhone

Infinitesimal

Pulled into the Arco gas station in rain to fill half-up.
Standing, pumping, I saw her crying, phone in hand.
Couldn't help but notice, and I tried not to, that the phone was wet too,
from her tears cascading down her face faster then the rain was falling.
Her mournful weeping easily dwarfed all the busy sounds
of that busy gas and food, stop and go place.
She talks a little bit and then cries some more,
punctuating by rapping her phone against her pump in obvious distress:
Bang, bang, bang. Trouble follows trouble follows trouble.
I find myself absorbed in this moist drama knowing my inclination
is avoidance of the sight of anxiety like this.
Something draws me. I don't think I'm alone here.
Seeing tears on strangers, don't you look the other way,
then back again?
She calms a little then asks a few questions.
"Please," she says, listens, then more crying, face red.
She fishes into a black shoulder purse for Kleenex.
I think she's tied to the world by her thin cell,
and getting the idea that being an adult is being alone.
Wondering about how much bad news
this insensible puny phone has heard in its life,
before I know it, I've put more gas in than I wanted,
having it sucked into the tank, startling and waking me up.
After putting hose back and getting receipt, I sit briefly in my car
steaming the rain dropped windshield,
staring out at that damp wounded person out there.
Her shoulders shake in symphony with her sobs.
When she rapped the pump did the dial tone switch to the present
and did his (it must have been) voice insist on breaking up?
Was it going to cost her?
But she continues wiping that flood of tears off her cheeks.
Doesn't she know the greatest hurt is what she does to herself?
I turn on the ignition, warming the engine,
and hot jazz pours out of the radio.
Nudging out into the crowded side street,
I leave her lonely figure behind in the rear view mirror
knowing if it wasn't for rain, the sun wouldn't feel so good.

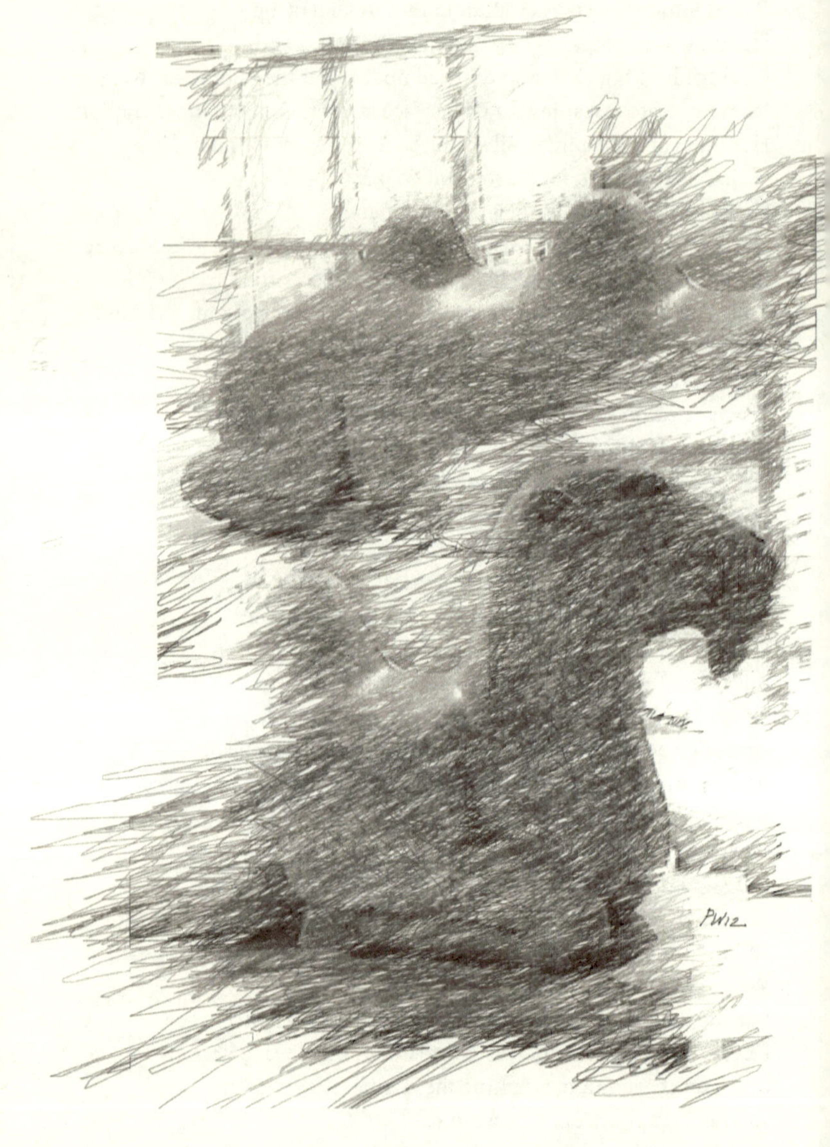
PW12

Advice for Future Artists

Looking up at the paintings,
he said he liked to draw too.
Maybe seven, maybe eight,
his size and age didn't hold him back.
Talked right up.
Wanted to know how much artists make.
Very adult. Wanted to know,
was I rich?
Had to tell this little kid
I didn't have a lot.
Doing all right though.
Doing what I wanted.
That's what mattered, I told him.
He smiled like he understood.
Then he turned and walked away
like he knew where he was going.
Just a little kid!
Out of nowhere I see I and my sisters his age,
hand in hand with Grandma.
We're walking on a broad concrete walkway.
Ahead, two marble camels, one on each side,
lie at the end of the walk.
Grandma lifts us up on one.
I sit between the sculpted humps, thrilled.
I swat the stone and click between my teeth.
It just sits there silently
but in my imagination we're moving, approaching dunes.
Never forgot that first day or the following ones
when I knew I'd be seeing them again.
Associated them with that old art museum they graced.
Happy for them too, when they moved them to the new one.
When I go up the stairs past them now,
I see the cool stone between their humps.
It's been worn smooth.
How many of us did it take to do that?
See, I say to myself,
imagination is so powerful it can wear stone smooth.
Should have told the little kid that.

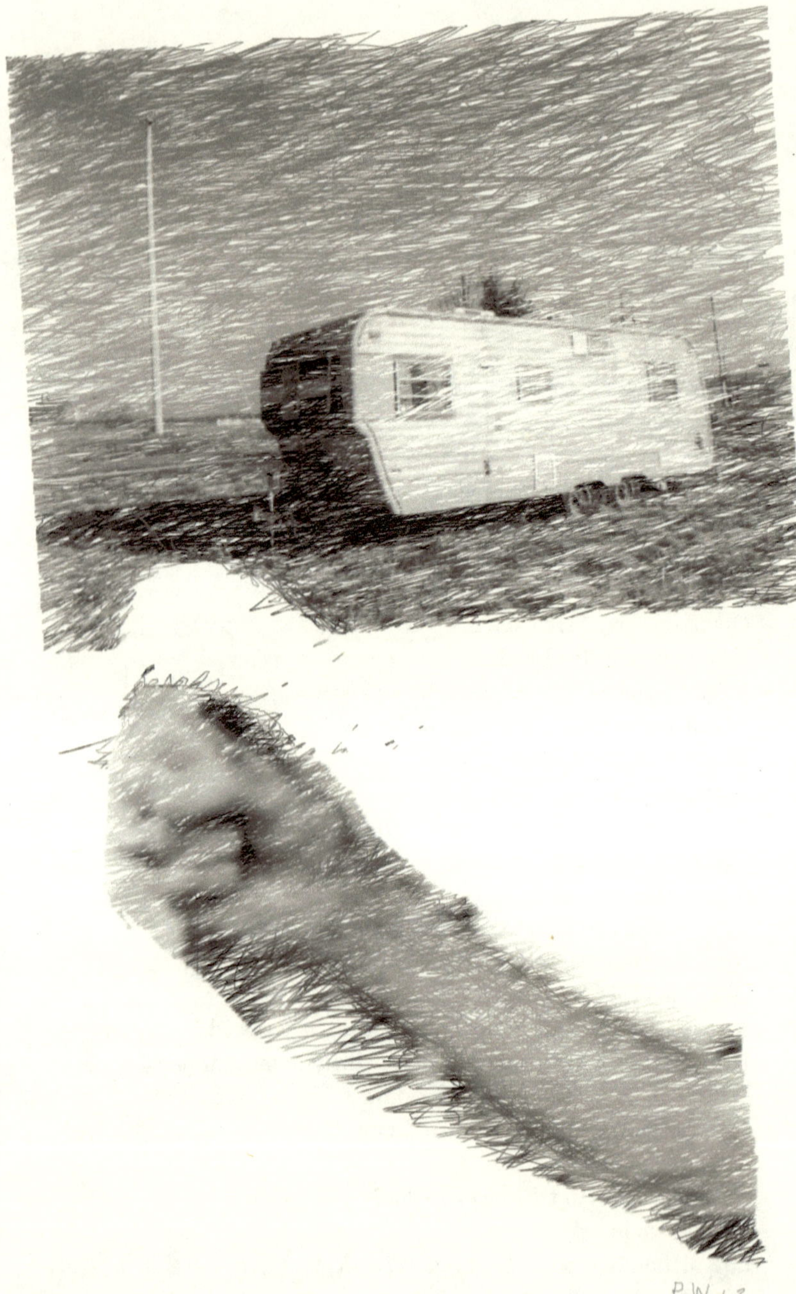
P.W 12

It Throws Itself at You

The wind always seemed to roll over the fields like it looked for you.
Ahead of its dust clouds the tumbleweeds ran separately
or bunched together until they piled into barbed wire, caught.
Mountains of them formed, especially in the corners where fences joined.
Waves of them formed those mountains in there.
And there was no getting away from the wind.
It cut through the trailer.
A crack, and it got in and threw grit over everything.
Pulling covers over your head gave a little comfort, shutting the sound out,
but then you'd picture him yelling again.

Didn't I tell you Dummy, not to get the tractor stuck.
He spins the wheels, just digging them deeper into the mud.
Flicking the switch off, his hand continues an arc like it was lightning.
Jesus Christ! This is all we need. You Son of a Bitch'n idiot.
Digging under the tires with shovel, he suddenly throws it into the field,
wheels, and strikes you in the face with the back of his clenched fist.
Blood shoots out of your nose and your ears start ringing.
But you don't notice.
You only notice your humiliation in the surprise.
You can see he's surprised himself, and is already sorry -
it's in his eyes, wide open and staring in the sudden silence.
Says something about being sorry,
about not knowing what he was doing, and pulls his handkerchief out.
Says he didn't mean it - just went crazy or something.
Don't know what got into me, he says over and over.
The wind picks up sand, throwing it into the blood caking on your arm.
Some gets in your eye. Squinting, blinking, tears form.
He thinks he caused it. Puts his arms around you.

Laying under the covers now, you see this all over again.
You had never seen his anger like that before.
It scared you into silence but now your mind won't shut up.
It seems to harmonize with the whistling wind out there
and the scraping of tumbleweeds caught piling into,
and now jerking and rocking the trailer.

This ain't no lullaby though.

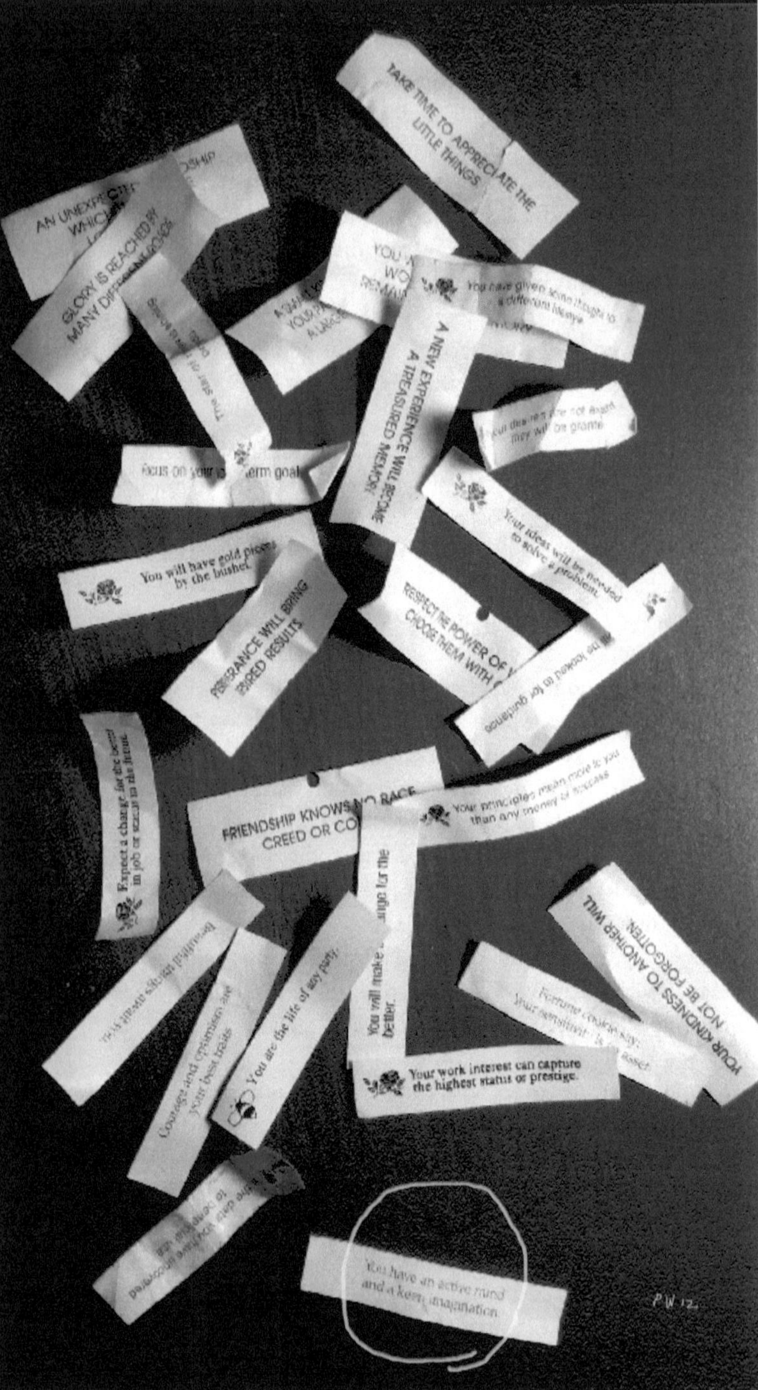
TAKE TIME TO APPRECIATE THE
LITTLE THINGS
You have given some thought to
a different lifestyle.
A NEW EXPERIENCE WILL BECOME
You will have gold pieces
by the bushel.
Your ideas will be needed
to solve a problem.
Expect a change for the better
in job or status in the future.
Your principles mean more to you
than any money or success.
YOUR KINDNESS TO ANOTHER WILL
NOT BE FORGOTTEN.
Courage and optimism are
your best traits
You are the life of any party
Your work interest can capture
the highest status or prestige.
You have an active mind
and a keen imagination.
P.W. '12

Chance Encounters

It came to the surface
blowing air in a large exhale.
Slick wet hair glistened
with the striking of the sun.
It's large seal eyes, black, stared.
I stopped paddling
and the kayak glided quietly
through the blue,
the green reflected Madroñas,
and the small diamonds
of smooth sunlight.
Staring back, I wondered
what flowed through its mind.
Was I another animal
spread here on the water,
covered in sun?
Its eyes begged knowledge.
Could probably see
something of me I couldn't.
They questioned in the silence.

Today, walking in rain,
one of my dogs barked.
Following his eyes, I peered
from under my hood right into
the downturned sharp face
of an eagle perched atop a pole.
Gave it thought.
Heard questions again.

While writing this out,
a scrap of paper on my desk
suddenly captures my attention.
Have to turn it over, see what it is.
From a fortune cookie,
it says, "You have an active mind
and a keen imagination."
Finally, we have an answer
to all those questions.

Coming Out of Dream

Every morning without fail
they're waiting for me
as I open the bedroom door.
Then their tails furiously wag
until we set off for our walk.
Ears up and bright pink tongues
hanging from perpetual smiles -
there's a lot I admire in them.
Coats always on,
I have only to fasten leashes
to their simple collars
and they pull me off
following trails of scent
of who knows what.
Their only concern seems to be
an intense interest in
leaving theirs behind.
Like canine loggers
blazing a trail with their marks,
we stop and go,
sputtering along toward rising sun.
On our right is Puget Sound
where I've heard Orcas' numbers
are growing fewer and fewer.
They're thinning out
and some believe they indicate
what's in-store for us.
I suppose at some point it's possible
that these dogs' trusting eyes
will be the only ones
staring back at mine.
That's what they'll get
for considering me
all-knowing and supreme.

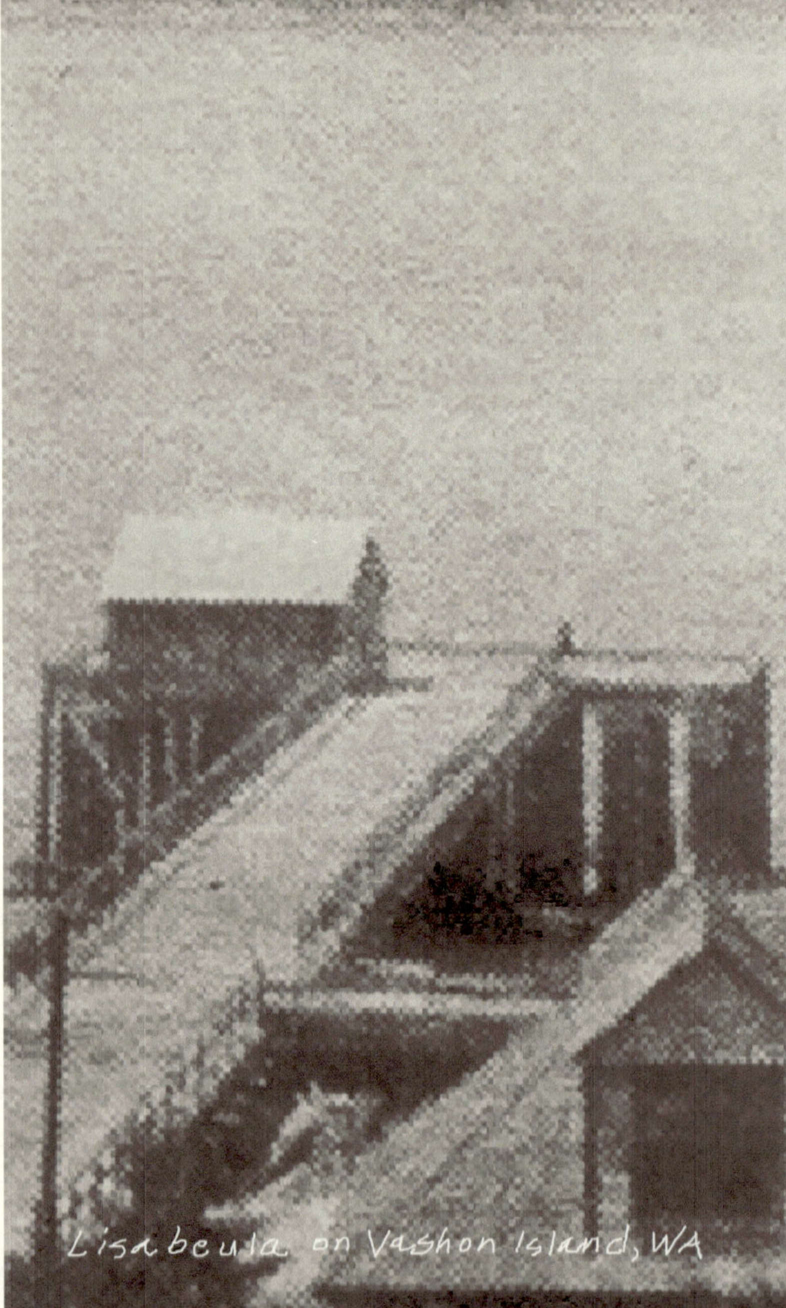

Lisabeula on Vashon Island, WA

Lisabeula

It lay at the end of a long dock.
Weathered dark gray and projecting into Puget Sound,
people occasionally had outings there.
Back in the old days when there were no roads
and people got around only by boat,
the boarded up stores and rundown hotel
with boardwalk connecting them, saw a lot more action.
When I was small I knew it as a ghost town.
My friends and I crawled around under the boardwalk
looking for old coins and bottle tops.
As the surf pounded the beach
we'd easily imagine any footsteps on the planks above
being made by fancy women and their suit vested partners
on their way into the hotel for some fun.
Laying on our backs in the sand
and looking at the bottom of the boards,
it was easy to make jokes
about something we knew nothing about.
We could picture the people though.
We'd seen some old photos.
We'd heard some stories.
One was about how the town got its name.
In order to have mail dropped off the passing boats,
the man who applied for the permit
was told the town needed a name. Official policy.
He couldn't think of one and asked the clerk,
who was staring at pretty secretaries,
if he knew any ... to help.
The clerk, mind elsewhere, said, "How about Lisa. Ahh, Beula."
This was the story anyway and we always laughed over it.
Once, laying down there, we heard girls coming
and peering through the boards, looked right up at them.
In those boarded over shadows, this secret had power.
On occassion now, I think of Lisabeula.
I think of the exposed grain of weathered wood planks
and will hear waves breaking on smooth stones.
I smell salt in the air and feel history's magic.
I see darkness and sense the loyalty engendered by seclusion.

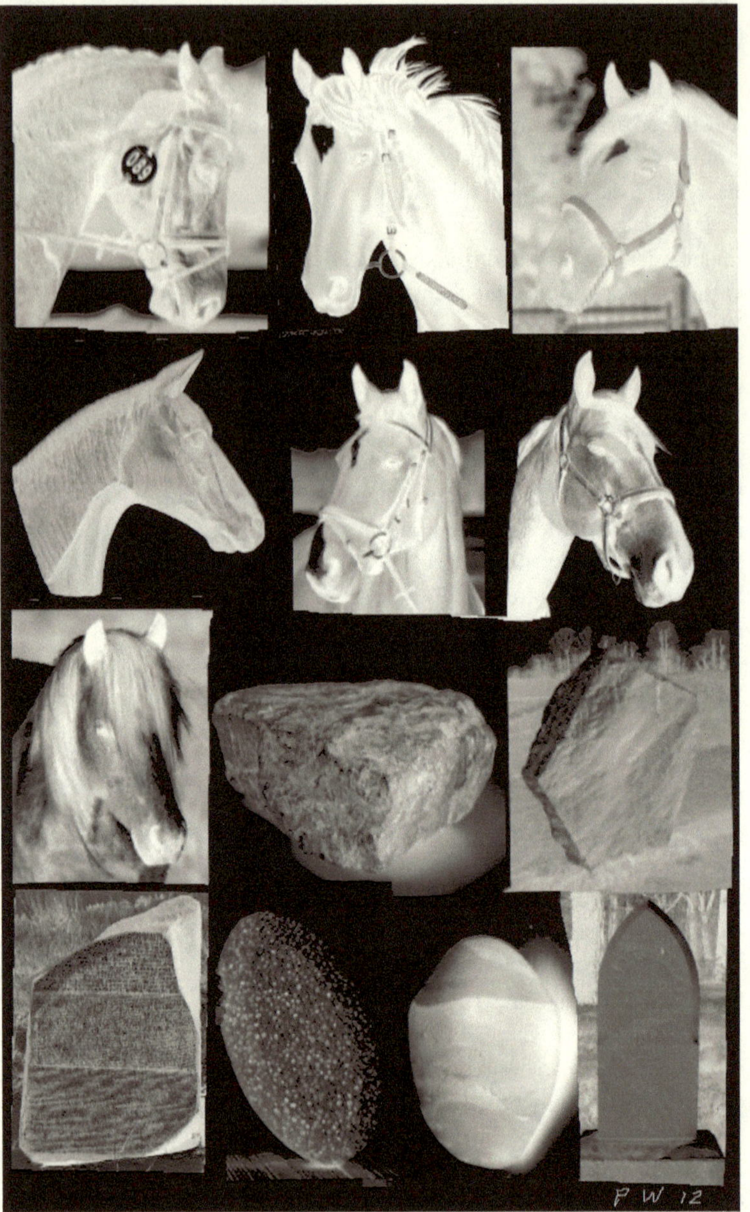
P W 12

Removing Word Blinders

I'm alone now.
Some close to me
have left my presence.
Feeling hollow,
like parts of importance
are missing,
I search in these lines
for them.
That's what a sentence is,
you know.
An old French word,
it means "to feel."
Constructing this poem,
lines and breaks,
one after another,
I'm beginning to realize
I always memorialize
those important to me.
It's how I throw
the light on them.
My horse sense says
I see better this way
and I need touchstones.
Emerson called them
masterpieces of nature
so it's funny
that in describing
friends' importance,
I've ended with
these old words.
Horses and stones.
Sense and touch.

Hunting Feeling

Home again
on the gravel path
out back

I look down
and barely have time
to jump

over the blood and fur
of something
ripped apart

with its guts missing,
just sprawling there,
driving me on

like an omen carefully placed
to make me feel
not welcome.

Piece by piece disappears
over the next few days
until there's nothing

to tell it was there,
saying, it pulled itself together
and ran back into the night.

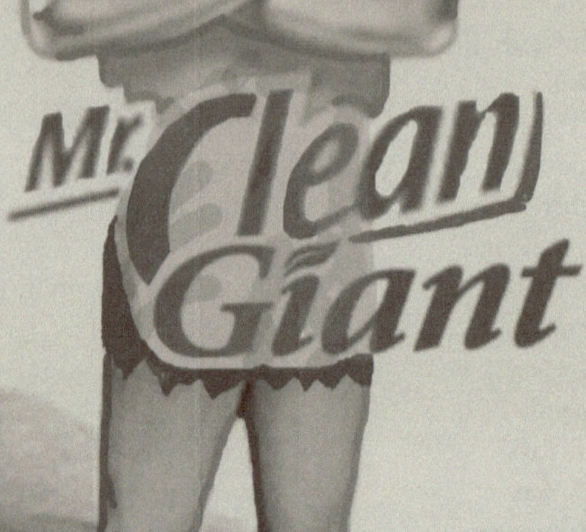
Mr. Clean
Giant

Whipped Into Shape

Nearly the first of February and the sun is shining.
It's like spring!
I feel energetic like a busy elf.
Become ball of energy.
Gather dog/cat hair.
Toss into wood stove.
Needs cleaning too.
Look through sooty glass door at fire.
See caught up spider disappear.
Wish horror would.
Eyes glaze.
Look out window.
Smudge on glass near face looks absolutely huge.
So big, it covers view.
Dwarfs it.
Distant beach looks small, messy.
Sweep up.
Throw driftwood back.
See ridge across cove needs rearranging.
Tear down offending houses.
Shove grown trees into gaps.
Stomp on earth to hold in place.
Oops. Crushed some cars.
Oh well. Had to go too.
Whisk from picture with houses.
Flick away motor boats while I'm at it.
Spy telephone wires.
Rip out, pulling poles like vine connected weeds.
Toss away too.
Really moving now.
Smoke curling up draws attention to jet trails.
Mar perfect cloudless sky.
Suck up like vacuum cleaner.
Standing now, hands on hips like jolly green giant.
Defy anyone to mess up.
Ho, ho, ho. Let's keep it clean, I roar, laughing.

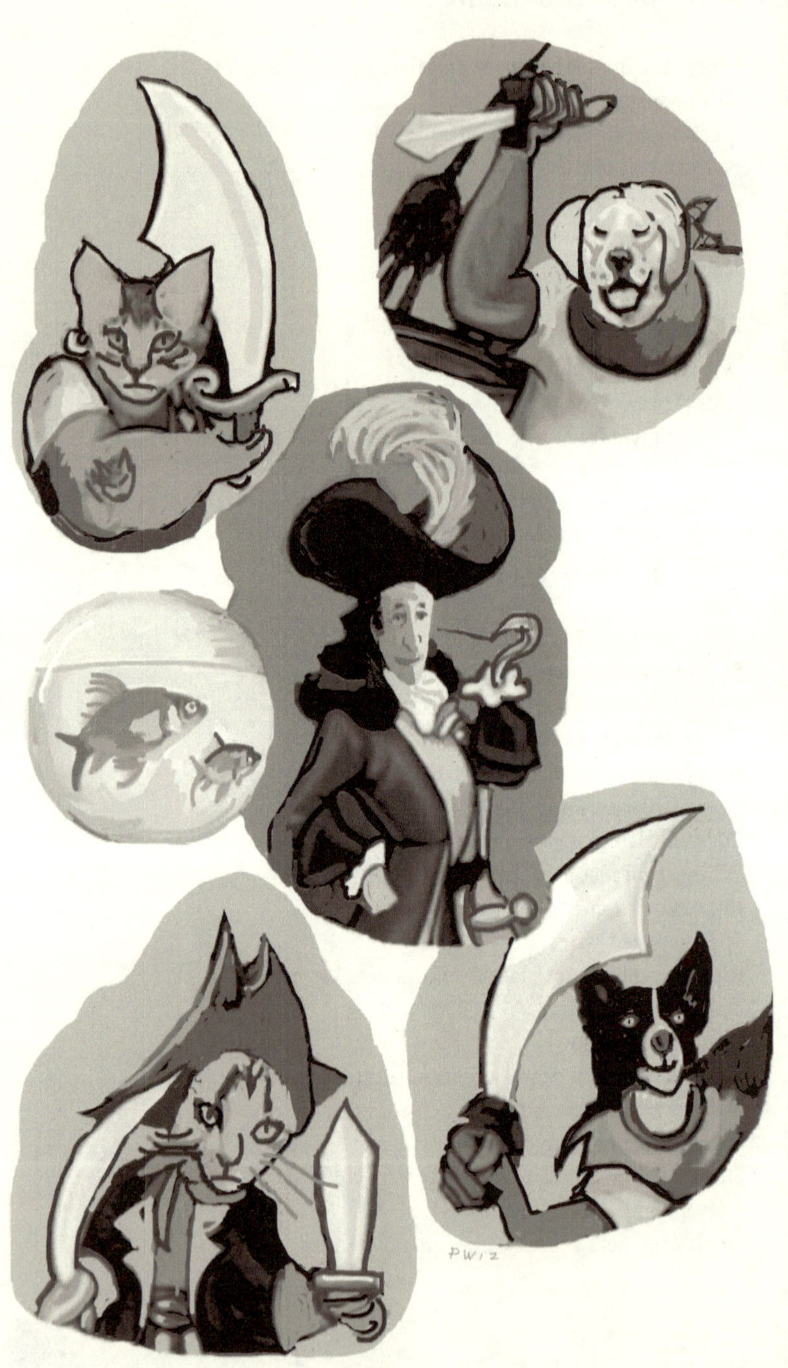

Sailing

Eagles float by scouring the beach for prey.
Waves pound.
A terrible wind sends litter flying past the corners
and into the glass, like the house is afloat,
crashing along in an ocean of stuff
that unknown sailors have not battened down.
It can get scary.
Sometimes though, I look out there and see all this seething,
this agitation and restlessness, flowing.
Then it becomes mesmerizing, something amazing;
really something quite beautiful.
Invariably, someone walks by on the cove road,
breaking the spell, sending the dogs crazy.
They bark like mad.
They don't allow me to hear anything.
Can't even think sometimes, all this howling flying in my face.
In here I'm alone with them, my cats, and my fish.
They contribute to a small on board population,
keeping me busy.
Like the howling, I try to quell all their little insurrections;
try to maintain discipline and subordination.
Should know their places, you know, or we'll lose direction.
All traces of civilization could be lost.
Oh, oh! Look sharp there mates. Weeds dead ahead.

Death of a Salesman

Yakety-yak,
do-or-die,
the ad man wheeled and dealed
with only a ghost of an idea,
raising the devil
and playing footsie
with one foot in the grave;
a sales slip
while running into the ground.

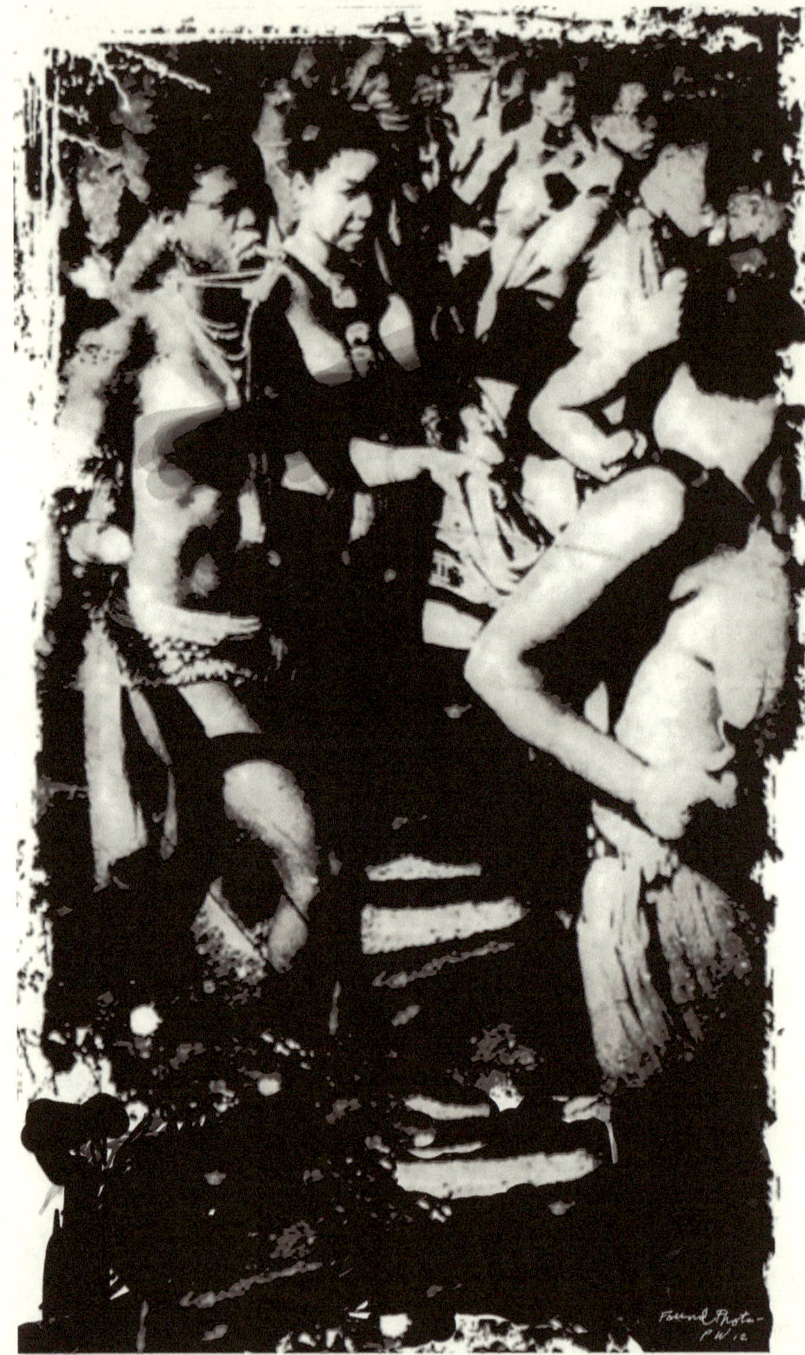
Found Photo-
PW 12

Wears Thin

Here in the Northwest, churches are everywhere.
Almost as many as taverns.
Can't fix it by praying, forget it by drinking they say.
This all started not that long ago
when pioneer missionaries saw all those natives they could convert,
a ready audience to preach gospel to.
Numerous like nuggets in a stream,
guess the gold rush in souls is still on
cause every time a person goes to turn around,
seems another church crops up
on what used to grow wild blackberries.
That's OK. People need places to pray
for all their co-dependents.
And they get really worked up about it. They do.
Reach right out and go door to door.
Anything really, to lead those that lost the path, the correct way.
Back into the fold.
Unfolded a National Geographic from the library the other day.
Leafing through, an old photo captured me.
Caption said it was "maidens en masse...
with king's right to choose another wife from the maidens."
Wasn't what caught me though. What caught me was
someone covered these women with a magic marker.
Really labored at it.
You can see this when the light shines just right.
You can see where the ink dried in pools
and the pools are real thick over their breasts.
Whoever did it must have felt
even people in photos are ripe for soul claiming,
ripe for correction and guidance.
No more flashing for them.
Real sloppy, the artwork looked like the artist was drinking,
maybe after realizing that the prayer wasn't working.
Then realizing drink wasn't either, resorted to using ink.
Powerful stuff, ink.
Just the smell of print on a page can make me drool.
Those of us that worship knowledge
can get really carried away too.

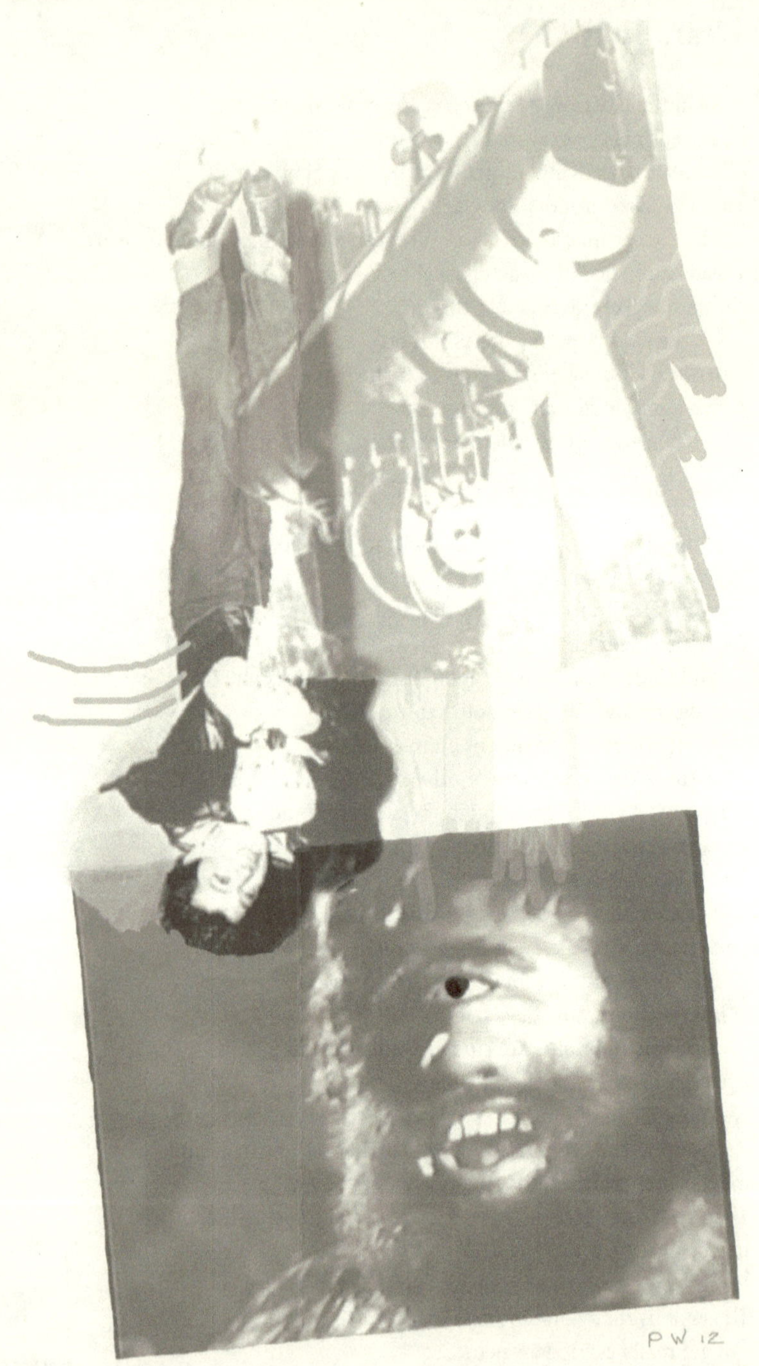
PW 12

Seeing Stars

I was upside down hammering
when the head of the nail
shattered and entered, sticking in my eyeball
like that miniaturized submarine
in the movie, "The Incredible Journey,"
or something titled like that,
where after being reduced to microscopic size
these people are shot through a syringe
into this guy's body to kill
some invading germs or something.
He was an important man I think,
like a dying company executive or something.
They end up coming out, surfacing,
out the corner of one of his eyes
and that's what I keep thinking about
after two days when I've tried every trick known to man
like Tony Curtis in a Houdini contortion
and the damn thing is still embedded in there somewhere.
My friends start holding seances
and swaying and crying
for me to go see a doctor.
Was I the man in the iron mask?
I began wishing I was, so I could be spared
the need to move my eyes,
which I did, unconsciously causing intense pain.
I felt like Cyclops must have felt
when Kirk Douglas rammed
that sharpened log into his eye
and he screamed and writhed
all over the floor of that dark cave
while pigs and men were running everywhere
trying to get out of his way -
watch out, this god has gone bonkers
for Christ's sake.
Didn't take much convincing
and I was waiting in Emergency
for the first available doctor.
Beat the Clock wasn't playing on the TV.
Time had slowed. *(Continued on next page.)*

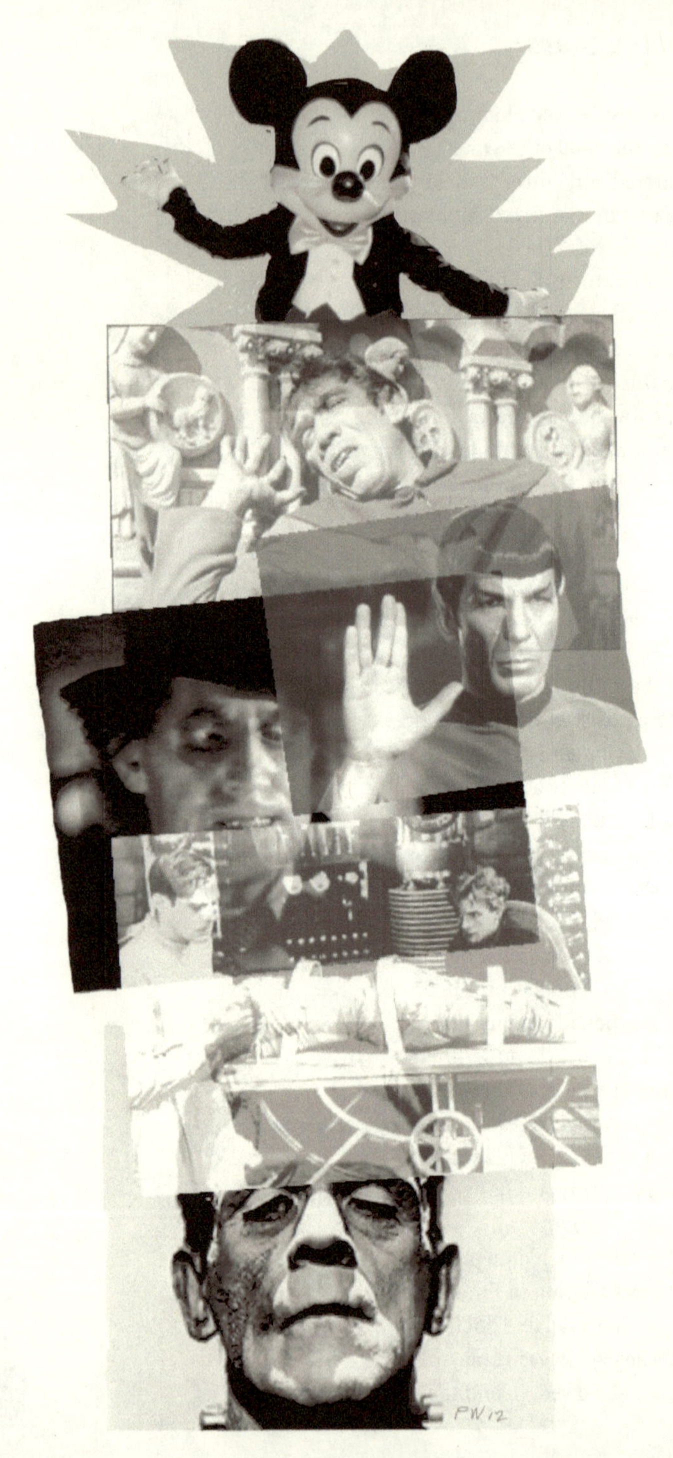
PW12

Finally a doctor and his student arrived.
The examination began.
Mine or the student's, I didn't know which.
The doctor asked where the foreign object was
and while I'm struggling to answer the student blurts out,
right over there, pointing kind of (watch out for the sharp log).
The doctor explains that the proper answer
is to regard the eyeball as a clock face
and then the object in question
is described as located at nine o'clock.
Is this Mickey Mouse, or what?
I felt Anthony Quinn hunch his back
hanging there from the clock tower face
as my body became flying buttresses
and all I wanted was the doctor or student,
I didn't care which, to pluck Anthony,
the dial, the face, the buttress, whatever, off.
Doc said I needed someone with more skill,
sending me on another quest in a neighboring hamlet.
The crowd that's gathered below
gets unruly and murmuring starts up.
Simple flutes play off screen.
A few hours later I'm beamed aboard at the other hamlet,
stretched out on a flying gurney,
and told Mr. Spock would be by shortly.
He's making his rounds,
the admitting nurse says apologetically.
Sure enough, Spock as Spencer Tracy comes onto the scene.
This time, twenty students trail.
He asks them calmly where the foreign object is located.
I'm feeling like Frankenstein's creation,
about to get shot with lightning bolts or something.
To speed things up, Van de Graf machine be dammed,
I blurt out that it's located at nine o'clock.
His Jekyll becomes Hyde as he looks down saying in astonishment,
that's the most impressive coordinated human response
I've ever seen in my entire history as a doctor.
The students lean back and gasp.
I'm Boris Karloff, a hideous suffering creature,
and I'm wavering between good and evil
(Continued on next page.)

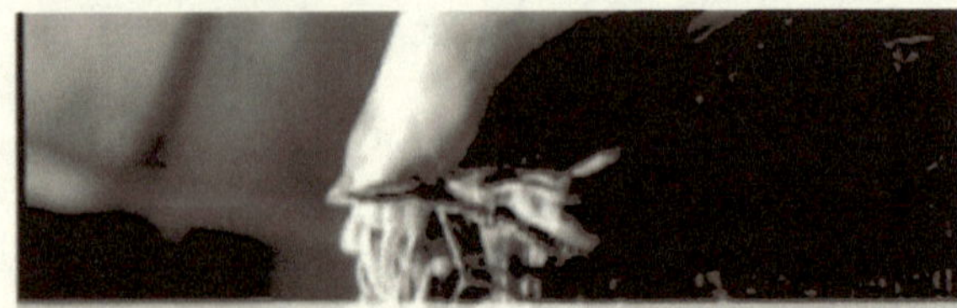
THIS, IN ITS OWN TERRIFYING WAY, IS A LOVE STORY.

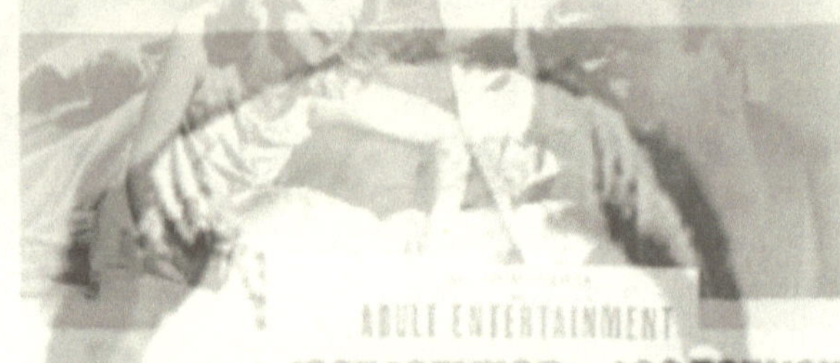
ADULT ENTERTAINMENT
JACK LEMMON
LEE REMICK
DAYS OF WINE AND ROSES

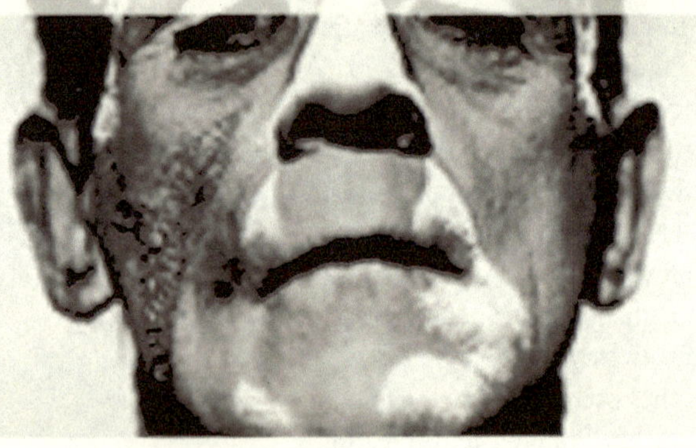

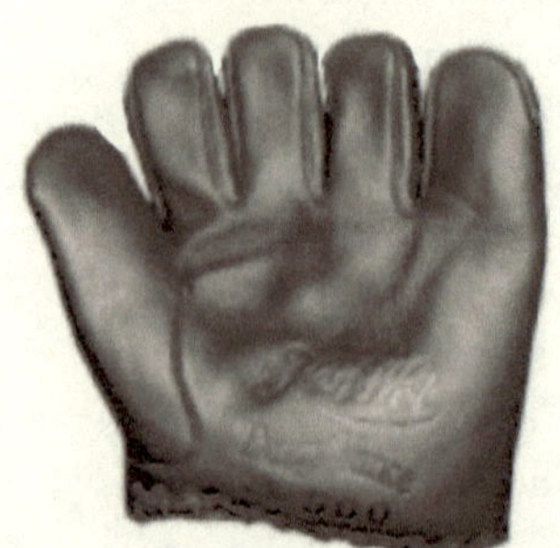

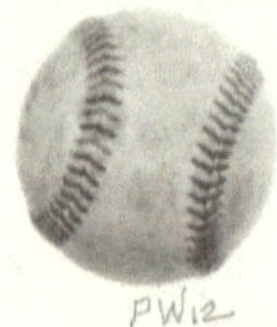
PW12

getting ready to kill my creator's lecture
if he doesn't pluck this sharp Alien's head out.
I think I see Sigourney Weaver in the back of the group.
My eye is, apparently, better as a clock. The alarm is going to go off.
One student, Lee Remick, slurs at another, Jack Lemmon, saying,
The days of wine and roses are over.
Dr. Frankenstein advances with an implement.
The sleeves of his coat brush over my face
and everything diminishes to black and white.

Sore Spot

I turned out for the baseball team when I was in junior high.
Proud, Dad said, Here, take my old glove. I used it when I was your age.
Gosh, the tradition of it all.
The smell of old leather and then memories and the thrills.
In the outfield under early evening lights.
The smells of dirt, grass, and sweat were always there
so that they're ingrained in my head now.
And of course, the smell of fear, of failure.
The first day out, I wore this pink shirt with gray piping.
When he hit the ball the coach yelled, This one's for you Pinkie.
He'd just instructed us in the finer aspects of lining up a fly
where you're suppose to sight it through the webbing
between the glove's thumb and fingers.
The ball socked right through.
Hitting my eye, it broke my glasses.
Preoccupied with my fear of not being able to perform I'd forgotten
that this old glove didn't have webbing between thumb and fingers.
I wore that black eye for weeks but never put that pink shirt on again.
Forty years later I can recall that hardball's touch that night.
Its only sign is a scar running through my eyebrow.
Still lingering, however, is the sting that the laughter had afterwards.
Don't call me Pinkie again, I told the coach.

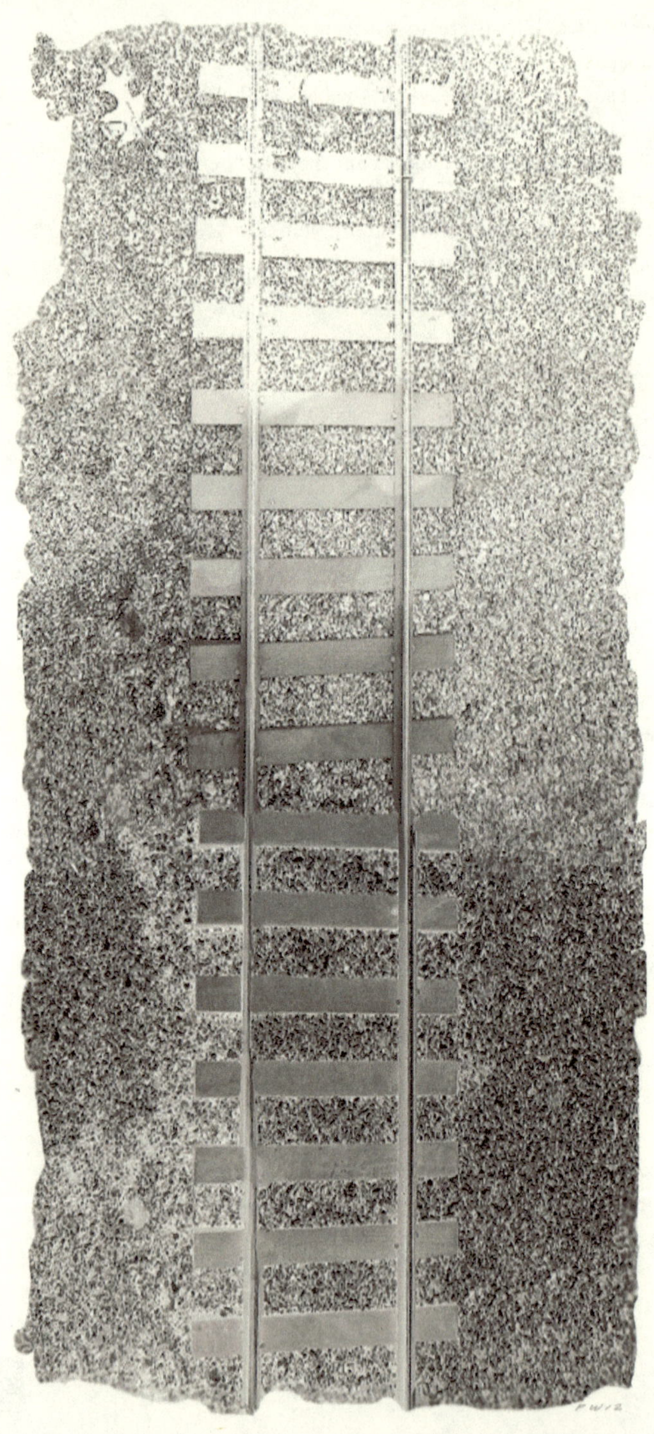
FW12

Prey on the Mind

Alongside railroad tracks that cut through grass and trees
was an old forgotten graveyard you found by accident.
You were checking out a pile of railroad ties
whose mound you spotted across the stubble of a mowed field.
At first you didn't notice the white stone slabs.
Under a tangle of blackberries and ferns they lay hidden and quiet; secret.
But the ties stood out, creosoted sides darkening
the sunny pale yellow horizon of the withered grass.
You thought they'd been thrown away; they weren't in a neat stack.
They were a criss-crossing mess bending the bladed shroud
of vegetation that they laid on.
You drove your pick-up over, loading them in back.
Afterwards, with the back of your gloved hand you wiped off
the beaded sweat that hung from your forehead like a curtain.
Smelling the pungent pig skin leather, your eyes suddenly focus
on something white smothered under the cover of a small knoll.
You walk over.
Spreading apart the undergrowth you see chiseled letters
whose once sharp features have eroded with time:
John Olson - Born 1803, Died 1847.
The slab next to him is his wife Emily. Born later, she died earlier.
Then you uncover the children's graves; four whose ages vary.
No epitaphs other than the barest facts cover the pitted marble sheets.
It's a family resting spot.
Stuck alone out there in the middle of nowhere, you wonder about them.
Sun setting, you jump behind the wheel and drive away,
the truck swaying heavily with its load.
Those ties make a great path through the woods to your front door.
You bury them into the mud,
their tops providing a weathered smooth walking surface.

It's been years ago but you've never forgotten that loneliness
out there under the dark green; the Olsons just lying there.
And every time the wind whispers, carrying the mournful toll
of a distant train whistle under its breath,
you question whether those ties were missed at all. You can't help it.
Your mind connects railroad accidents to graveyards.
It has plagued you ever since.

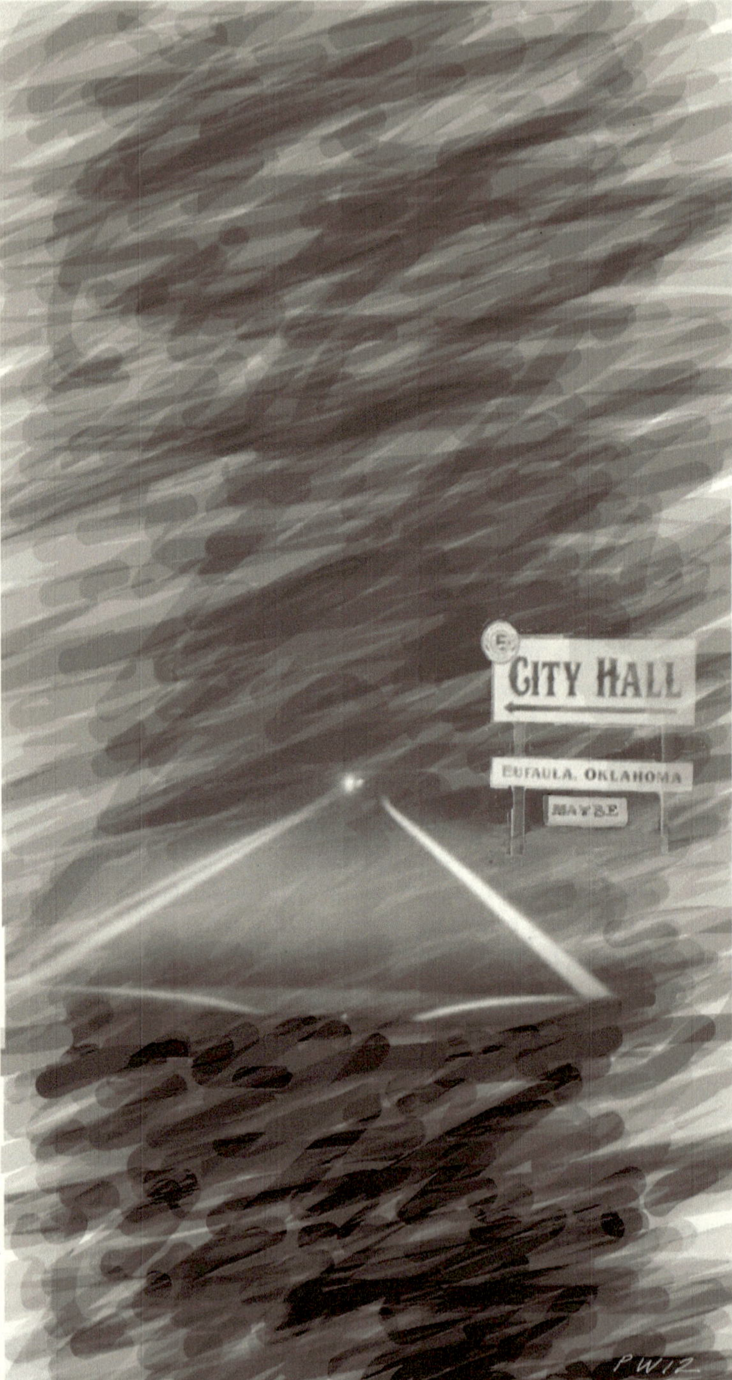
CITY HALL
EUFAULA, OKLAHOMA
MAYBE
PW12

Toying With the Familiar

After visiting friends, at the end of the day we'd leave.
I'd fall asleep in the back seat without trying.
Playing cowboys and Indians all day was taxing
and without fail, the car would always do this to me.
Maybe it was the humming of the tires.
Maybe it was the sense of safety under the blankets.
Then something, maybe going over a pothole, would wake me
and the car's dashboard would be silhouetted in front
by the headlights that raced ahead on the pavement.
They stared straight into the black night, silent and stoic.
Next to my two sleeping sisters, I'd peer out from the covers
and in my half-sleep, everything always looked familiar,
being coated with and leveled by the darkness.
I would think that home was just around the bend,
over the approaching hills that loomed up,
or through those trees whose shadows branched wild just ahead.
I allowed this feeling to toy with me and linger for miles
for it had a strange comfort in it which I'd try to hang onto.
I never did. I'd always drift back into dreams.

I live now on a highway, straight as an arrow about one half mile
after passing some buffalo fenced in a corral.
You can recognize it. It's where piles of old timber,
an upside down sink, and rusting old cars lie.
And the house itself?
It's got peeling paint and tar paper being torn off by the wind.
My father told me the other day that he was passing by
and a traffic construction project stalled him right out in front.
He had looked over and his immediate thought
was that he'd seen better on the reservation.
This gets me going.
Now I can't help but wonder if any Indians passing at night,
when the moon isn't hindered, look over and recognize things.
There is a certain amount of the familiar in this.
Blood of the Creek Nation passes through me.

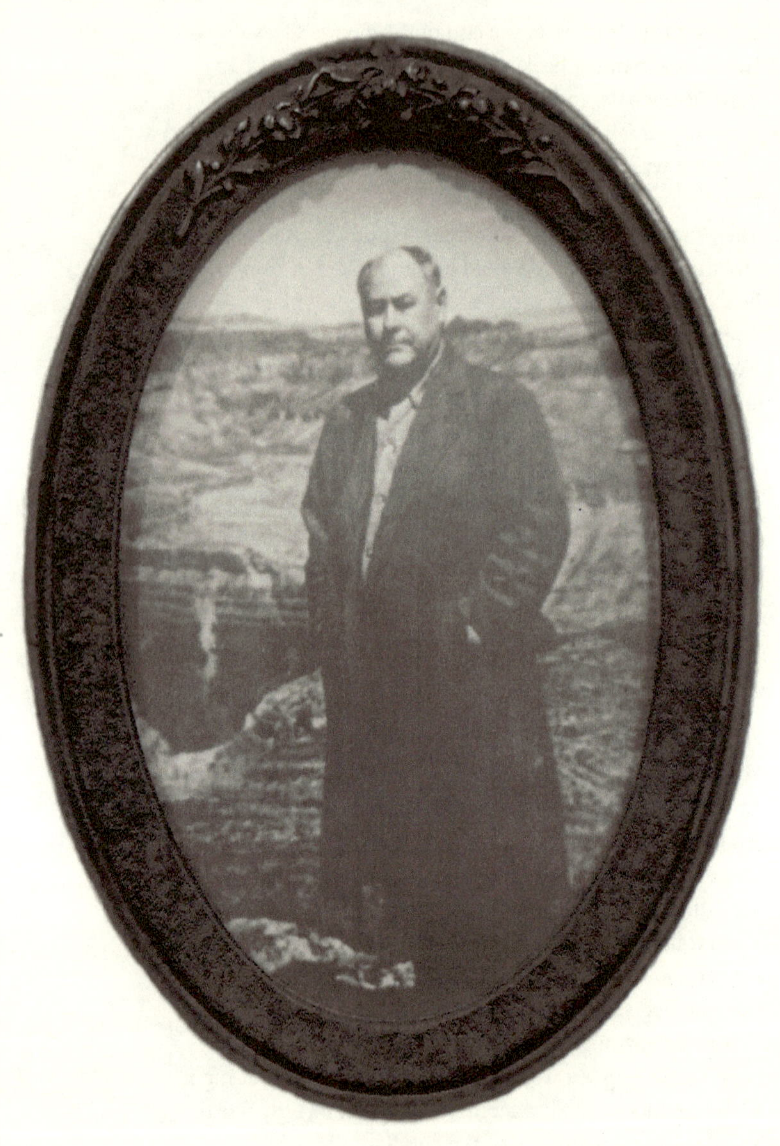

Admiralty Head

The dead that went before us
seem to grow dimmer with time.
What we see in front of us now
becomes easier to know,
brighter and unfaded.

I stand on this wind beaten hill
and look out across the Admiralty Inlet
wondering how many
this lighthouse helped save;
how many were caught in its old beacon.

I call it the Fort Casey Lighthouse, which it isn't.
I call it this because I have ties here
and because that's where it stands,
white walls, red tile, black metalwork
stiffly at attention on green grounds.

A good 20 years before its birth
my Grandfather marched behind the big guns nearby,
a young Creek Indian from Oklahoma
who just wanted a cavalry horse.
The army brought him here for artillery instead.

I've read the love letters he wrote
to my Grandmother, a librarian from Seattle,
telling her he didn't want to be here
and how he felt out of place, wanting to get drunk.
They've brought me closer to him.

Standing here, the wind sighs in the evergreens,
wanting me to know more,
wanting me to return to my origins.

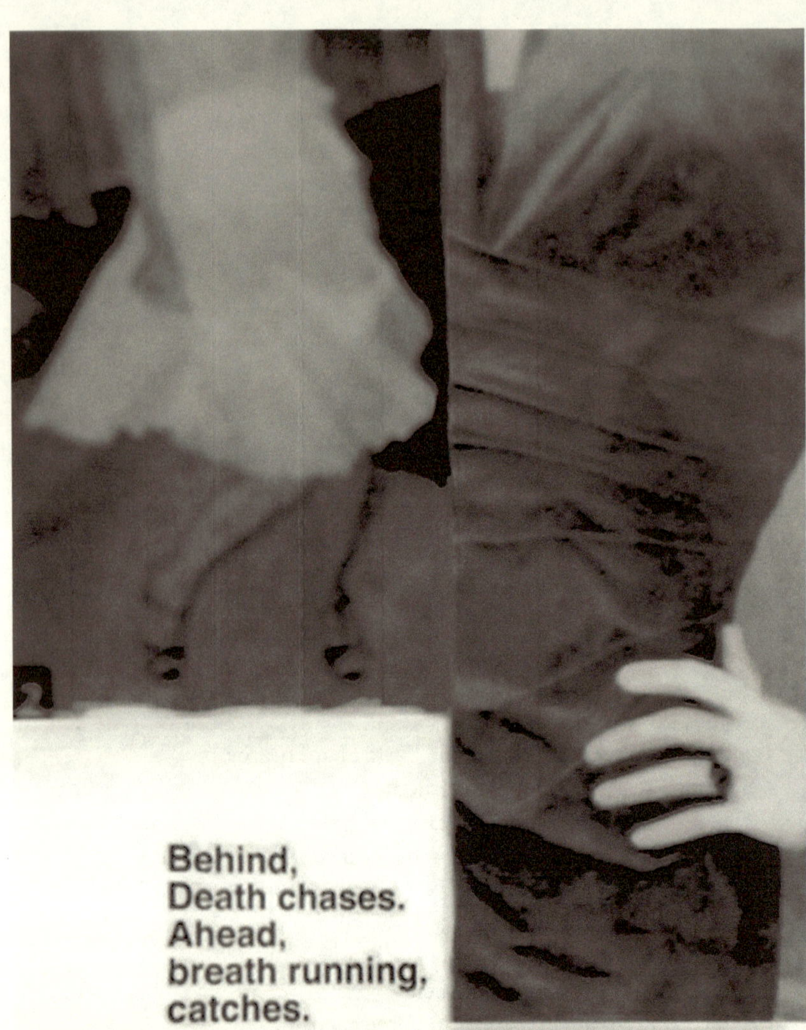

Behind,
Death chases.
Ahead,
breath running,
catches.

Ambition

Sometimes I want to, but can't. It just won't come out.
Sometimes I'm completely stymied about what it is I should write about,
especially if I haven't done so for a bit.
As I do every morning with coffee,
looking out the window, I thought about this.
My view is of a pretty cove in Puget Sound
whose sparkling water reflects the constant changes above its surface,
never failing to capture my attention and sometimes my pen.
Whether some gigantic old log stump floating out there,
flooded down a mountain river by melting snow pack,
or the sudden rubbery slick side of a gray whale as it dives
to sift the bottom for sand shrimp,
it's totally engrossing and a strong attraction.
It was surprising then when I'd found that this morning
my eyes had slowly settled to the ground under the bottom of the sill,
the ground that's close to the foundation.
Focusing, I saw this very small snail,
oh, let's say about the length of my thumbnail,
moving, it appeared, infinitesimally slow.
I watched it carrying its large shell, its shelter, on its back
as it inched along the stem of a weed.
Rain drops also shared that stem,
appearing as large transparent silvery boulders next to the snail
that they cascaded down alongside, stop and go fashion.
The snail nudged them like it questioned their existence.
Its antennae supporting dots, its eyes, moved, swaying back and forth,
watching in its world what I couldn't see in mine.
In its world, maybe its mind raced.
I have to admit that after studying it for a while,
it became larger and faster.
The relativity became apparent. And the mystery.
What is there in asserting control over the inconsequential;
in blindly marching forward based on what is nowhere but inside you?

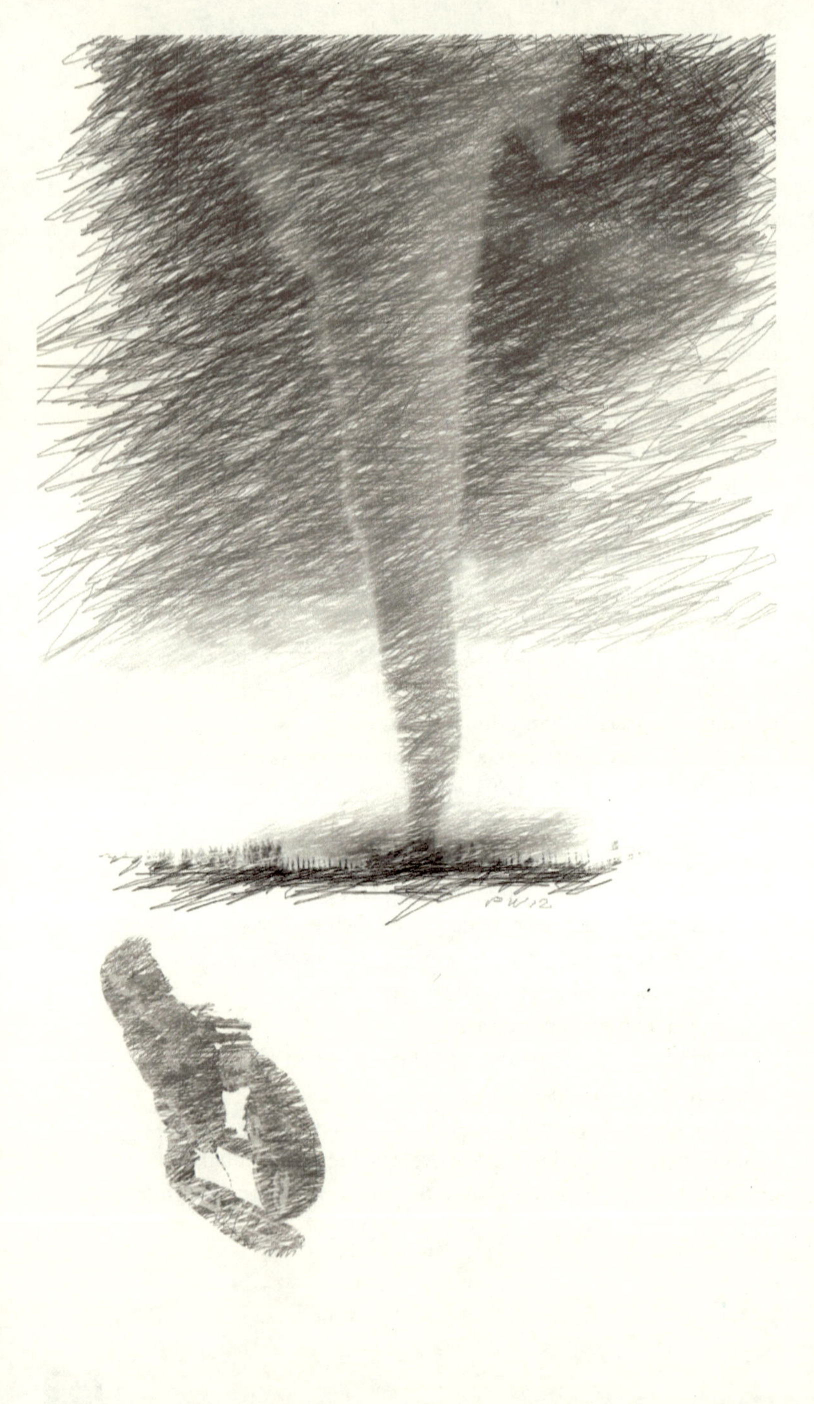
PW 12

A Living Picture

The man on the radio this morning told me
we're going to get gusts off the Strait at 55 miles per hour.
Out my kitchen window the ground tries to be sky
as neighbors' yards rush by along with odd bits of paper,
the litter of unknown passing strangers.
In here I'm faced with another piece of paper. It's blank.
I'd planned to paint a picture on it.
I avoid its stare and storm around not really doing anything,
feeling up in the air. Wind does that to me.
To settle down I've tried writing this.
Poetry channels my thoughts like air drawn through a filter.
Now I'm realizing that I'm trying too hard; preconceiving.
Good! I'm pinning myself down.
To paint a picture of some friends, I planned to suspend
a giant lobster over their heads, like it was swimming through air.
I wanted a model, spending hours fanning through National Geographics,
ones with "Maine" spelled out on their spines, calling like mockingbirds.
These calls are to no avail. Instead, time flew. My dream blows.
My perspective gets screwed and the wind's howling isn't helpful.
Looks like I'll have to throw another idea back.
I look over the hill at the water. The crashing waves look small
and rain drops running down the glass are huge.
Normal for someone who'd paint a lobster clawing air, trying to stay alive;
trying, like memory on the fly, passing out of the picture.

Fire Red

Tonight the sun is an explosive ruby
as it drops into rose tinged western sky.
My hands are warm and flesh pink with day's wear.
I zip my coat against the gathering fall cold.
Then you slip into mind and my lips part,
whispering your name, breath visible.
It's your name written with air by a heart
red with desire like a live coal.

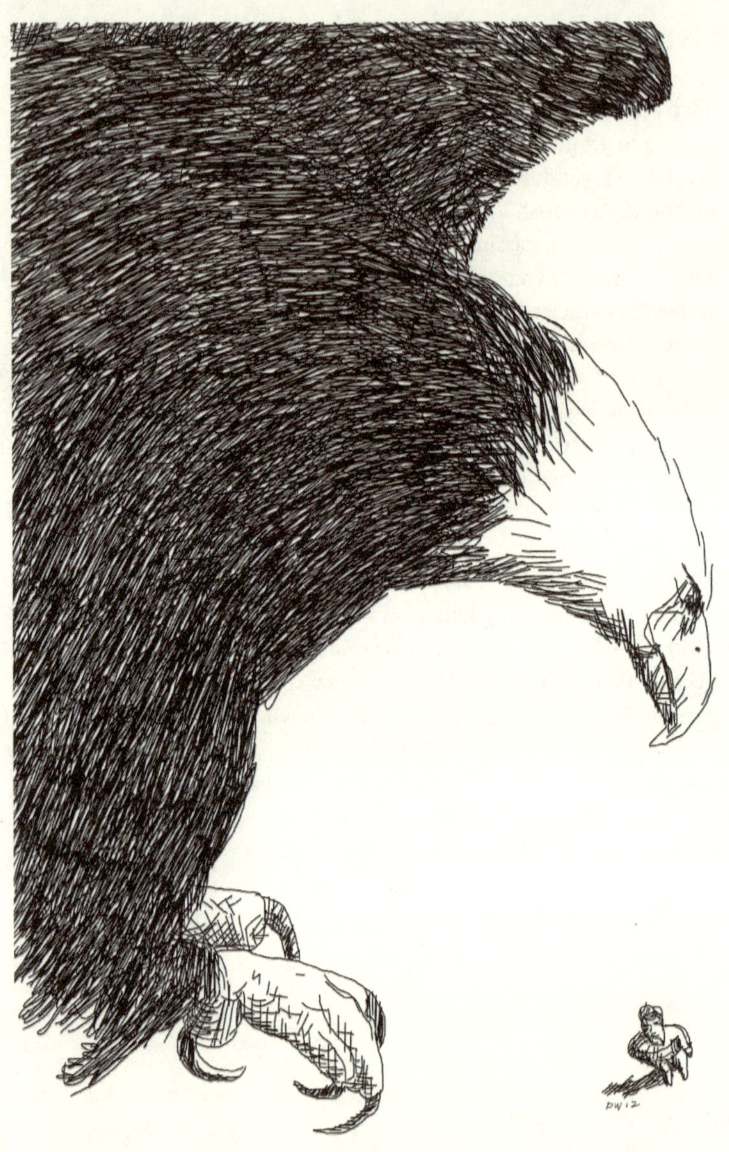

Eye to Eye

I scan the horizon over the sea
and watch some gulls wheel in the sky.
They're agitated and are fleeing off
to the east, following the bluff edge
where air currents rise sharply.
Their light gray bodies float by,
shearing off only now and then
to circle and circle, then continue.
They're watching and they're guarded.
And I see why! These huge black shapes
stand out with outstretched wings, gliding.
But they're more effortless. Two of them.
Big Bald Eagles striking fear into the beach.
Not just the gulls, but all the birds
move in front of them and seem to know
that dying goes with these two forms
that lack in warmth and are indifferent.
Their feathers so dark, so very black.
They soar over me and I see one
cock head and beak, swoop even lower,
looking, as if eyeing and studying me.
With hair and goose bumps rising,
I distinctly hear its high pitched scream
saying, "Freer, freer... freer!"
Is it admonishing me that it is, "Freer?"
Fear has such sharp eyes and ears.

Path of Least Resistance

In a straight line the trip went by too fast to be counted,
making it seem like it hadn't.
A blur, an out of focus snapshot taken,
it was like a dream you awake from, then can't for-the-life remember.
Good things go like that.
They disappear fast when you don't want them to
at the end of the line.

Entangled

By the time we got around to separating,
I only wanted to see her disappear.
She finally did, ruthlessly taking what she wanted
and driving it away in a rented U-Haul,
her lips tight and down turned, her face clouded.

At first, happy, I took to the radio for company.
One time I heard some scientists talking
about how they had always thought
that following the Big Bang, the universe was expanding.
At some point it would slow, stop, then collapse in again.
This didn't appear to be happening, they said.
Now, for some reason, it appeared to be
continuing to expand at a faster and faster rate.
They said it was caused by something unknown.
Mysterious, they decided to call it Dark Energy.

Eventually I discovered, even the radio didn't help.
The nights began to seem never ending
and that winter there were two kinds of light over Seattle.
Turning, restless, I could see stars, if the low clouds parted a little.
In the rain cleaned air they would sparkle,
set against the black space.
They seemed close like the memories of her voice
that with a start I thought I'd hear.
Crying out, I squinted to see better, heart beating full, rapid.
The only answer was my echo bouncing
off the frozen sides of the house next door.
They emulated disappointment in the silence of the night.

Then there were the house lights on the distant hills -
First Hill, Beacon, and even Cherry close by -
twinkling against the dark evergreen and the moving mist.
They seemed to merge with the stars above,
so that it was impossible to tell when sky and hill separated;
they had become parts of each other.
It made me think I was destined to continue letting things go
until I couldn't even find myself anymore.

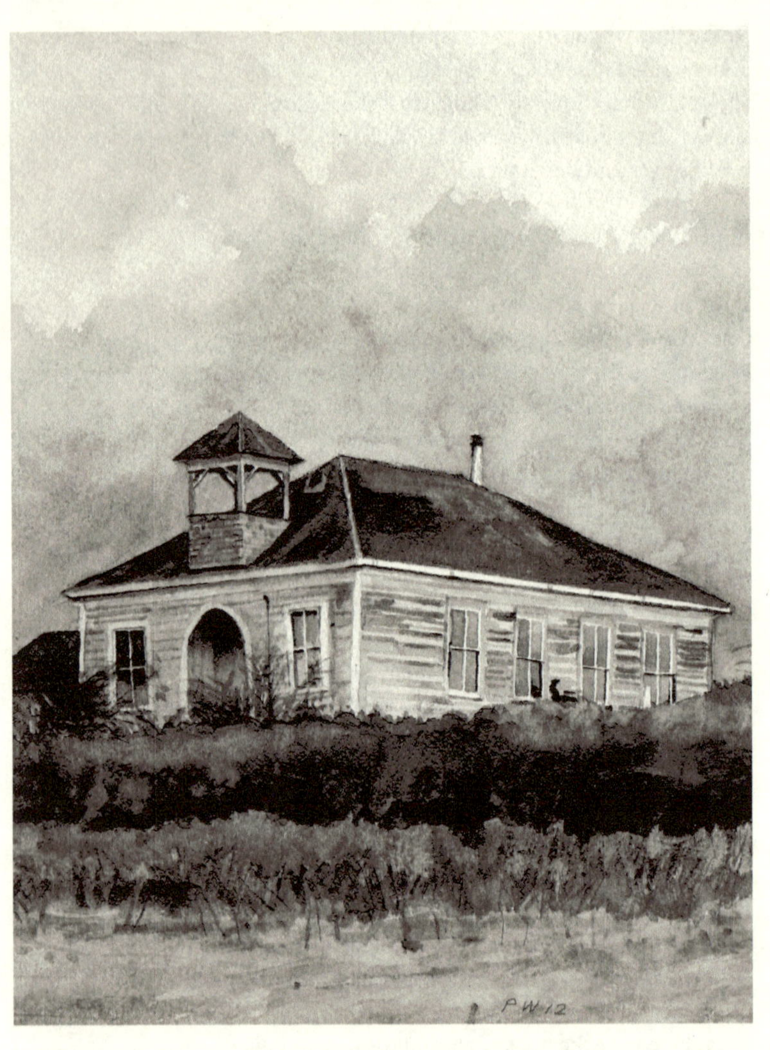
PW 12

With Gravity

My poetry comes hard for me right now.
Outside, ripe apples are blown from a tree onto a storage shed's metal roof.
In this pitch black night they tremble, find gravity, and dropping, hit.
The dogs bark thinking it's someone banging around trying to get in.
I can't hush them. I let it go.

I have let a lot of things go.
Sometimes accumulating, they come back and haunt me.
Like those apples.
I add them to the list.
I probably won't clean them up now,
but just being there, they bother me.
I have to say to myself I have other things to do right now.
So the list grows and as it grows I hold back more and more,
afraid that all the stacked up stuff will occupy me much too much.

I let a lot of things go this way.
They bother me but drop away when other things intrude.
Like the sound of the wind blown apples, it's upsetting.
I let my poetry go a few days ago.
Wanted to get some little things done, thinking it would come back.
It hasn't. I can't hear my own music now.
My guilt over small things drove it away.

Up on the hill above me
lies an old one-room schoolhouse.
In the wind there are only whispers through dry grass
where teachers once taught the spoken word.
There's poetry there in the quiet of the wind.
Maybe I can catch some again.

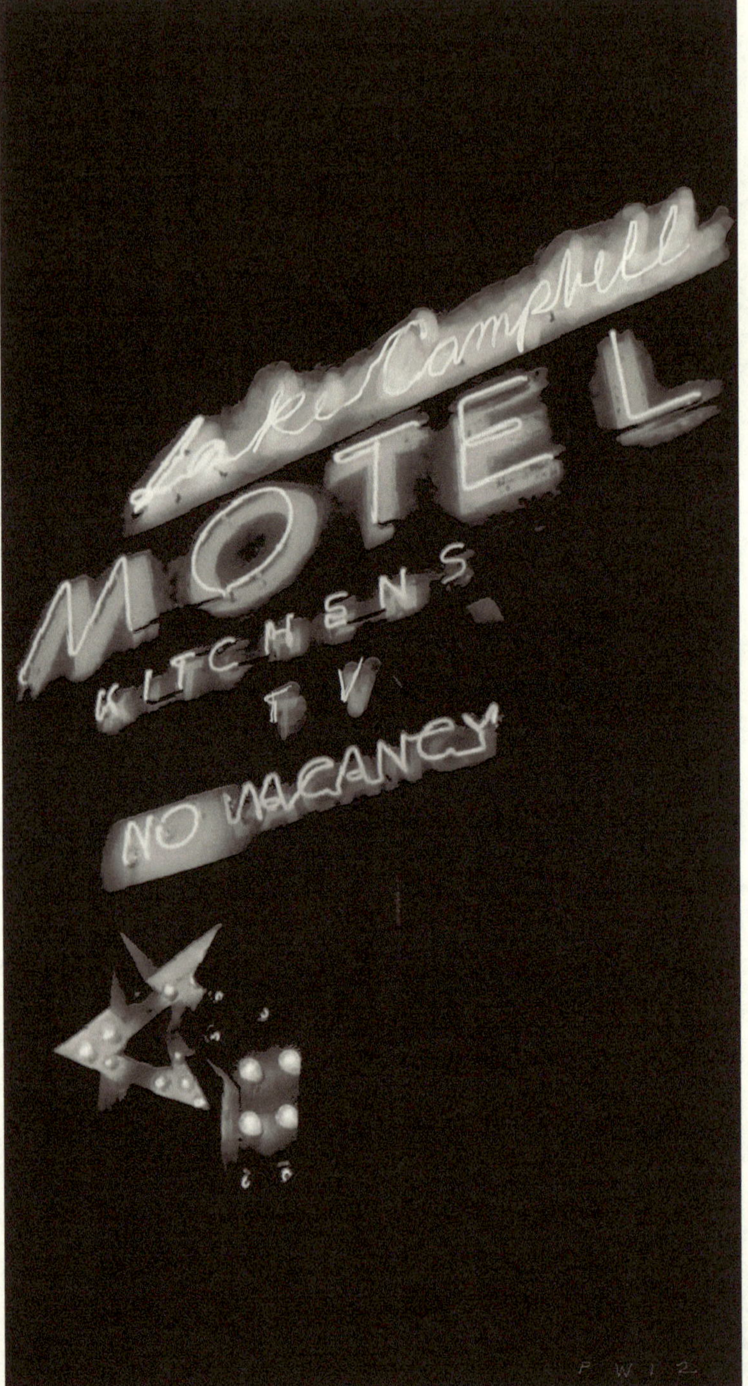
Lake Campbell
MOTEL
KITCHENS
TV
NO VACANCY
P W 1 2

Dear Dreamboat

I'm on the fly today. On the go.
Cruising here in a pack of cars.
Heading due north off-island for some supplies.
Still dragging my anchor though,
hoping to hook some poetry in the here and now;
something current.
I'm lost in thought, a bit foggy as I sail around this bend.
Hold it!
All of a sudden there it is ahead on the starboard side.
A real favorite of mine.
Lake Campbell Motel, the sign reads.
Vacancy.
And in smaller letters, Kitchens - TV !
Just a small unpicturesque grouping of motel rooms
across the road from a raft tethered just offshore.
Not much to look at, it always gets me when I pass by.
Does now!
Something romantic about its commonness.
Sends me somewhere else.

We meet. A rendezvous, the French say.
We leave the TV off.
Watch each other, concentrating on each other's eyes.
We kiss delicately, then harder, feeling for love and getting it.
We sleep soundly as others storm past.
We make and sip our coffee in the morning listening to the birds sing.
Warm some sweet rolls for our continental breakfast.
Then hugging, we part not knowing.

Up ahead I spy an old land yacht.
Stalled out at the light, it's steaming ironically across from a used car lot.
The owner is pounding madly on its roof, pissed.
Wakes me up doing sixty-five. I've been dreaming
and taking notes on the only piece of paper handy -
an old envelope that sits on the seat beside me.
Running out of space scribbling, weaving down the highway.
In the rear view mirror I see those following have pulled back.
They're giving me a wide berth.

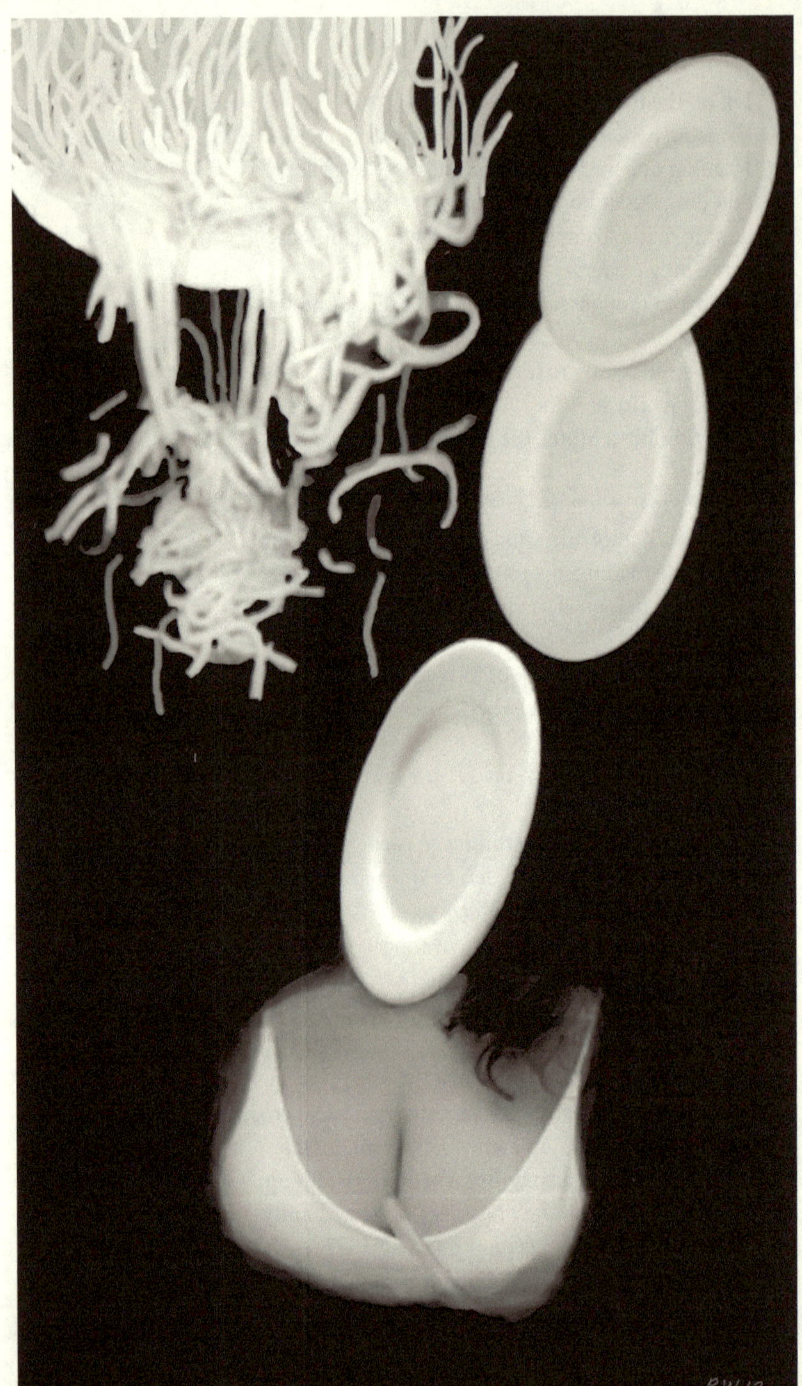
PW '12

House Boy Adrift

Using my back, I would open the swinging doors
separating the kitchen galley from the sorority dining room.
It was a barrier in more ways then one
between our sweating work and their stillness and quiet staring.
Entering, juggling plates, I felt their eyes on me like hands.
Made me uncomfortable, thinking every woman there, beautiful.
It made it hard for me to wait on them.
At dress dinners they appeared in low cut gowns
while I was all buttoned up in white coat, shirt, and black bow tie.
Served solids to the left, liquids to the right
and the cleavage between was hard to ignore.
Felt flushed most of the time.

The first time I went through those doors was to serve spaghetti.
Before doing that, the cook would wipe up
the excess tomato sauce it floated across the plate on.
Presentation was part of the meal, she spitted
before I voyaged out into that dining room.
Stiff backed, she sputtered like a pirate, which was often.
Threw pots and pans. Also, once, a knife.
Backing through those swinging double doors I prayed
the slip-sliding pasta stayed on the dishes, stacked three to an arm.

In their presence, clumsy, their eyes penetrated me like beacons.
Noting this, they toyed with me, moving to where I planned to set plates,
requiring contortions to sail around them.
They were like crags in front of the shoreline of the table.
Giggling to each other, their breasts jiggled like rolling waves.
Halfway around the table was the gorgeous Esther,
her bleached blond beehive hairdo, itself, both beacon and shoal rock.
Approach increased trepidation.
Crossing her arms under her chest, bulging it upward for my glance,
and smiling coquettishly at me, she leaned on one elbow
whispering something into the ear of the mate next to her.
Felt this one looking up too, laughing.
Concentrating on navigating between them, leaning in from left,
sauced pasta on right, unanchored, drifted down to bleached shoal rock.
Diminished, my red face, a new beacon, lit the room
trying to outshine bright red dripping beehive.

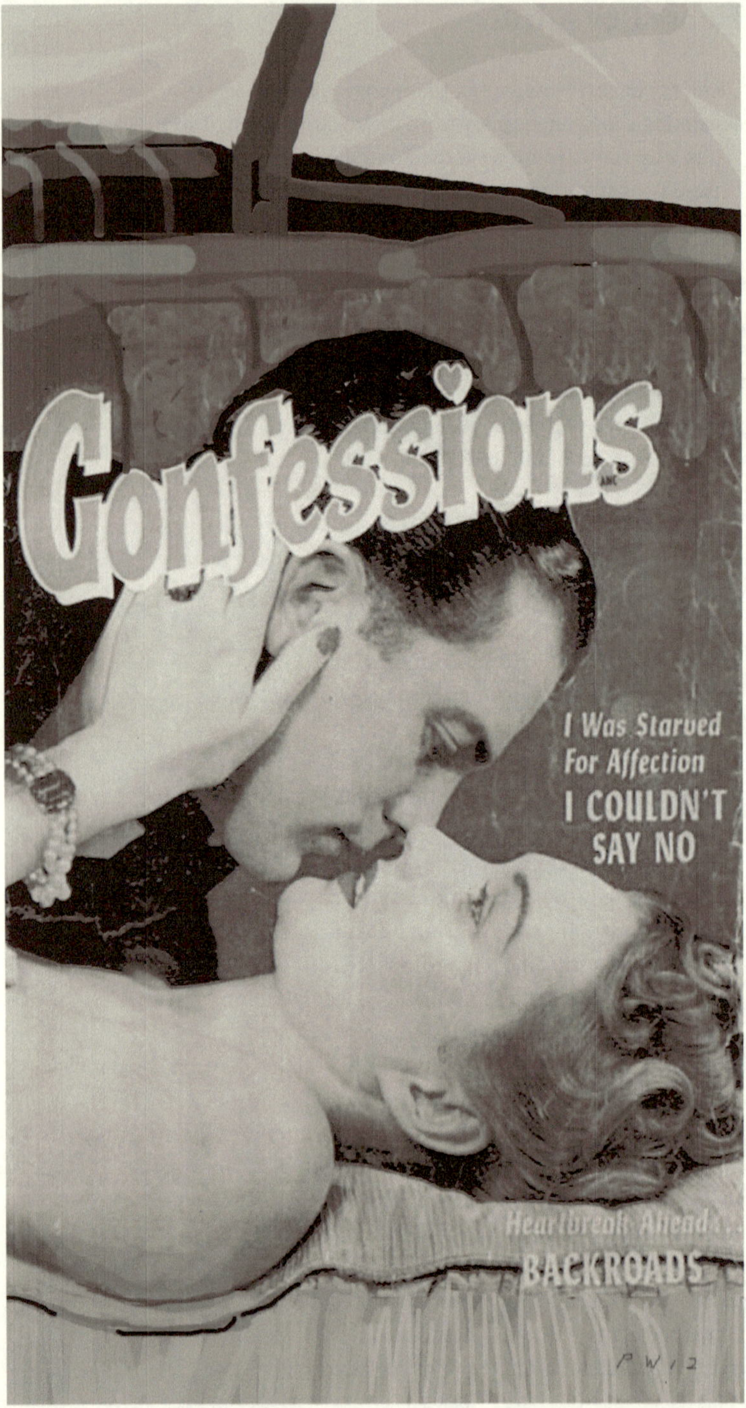

Confessions

I Was Starved For Affection

I COULDN'T SAY NO

Heartbreak Ahead...

BACKROADS

PW 12

Spirit

He tosses back a mouthful.
Peers at the label.
3 STAR Vodka. A Pint.
Says The Old Monastery Co. in Hood River is the distiller.
They're parked on a dark back road near the beach.
He passes it to her.
She takes a mouthful and passes it back.
She says she's nervous.
Never drank in a car before, she says.
He tells her she's beautiful.
The clear vodka disappears in the clear bottle,
a little each time it's passed.
The stars twinkle.
Her nerves are jumpy, not knowing what's coming.
He's directed but prays the vodka steadies his.
Tipping the last back, courage up,
he leans over and kisses her and she lets him.
She runs her hand around him, encouraging him.
He runs his around her. Drops the bottle.
Bound together, their lips touch.
She prays he's gentle.
He tells her he thinks he's in heaven.
She's his little angel. Says he worships her.
The bottle, empty, lays on the floor near the brake.
Label says 3 STAR Vodka. A Pint.
100% Natural Spirits.
It's a libation for their devotion,
but what's a monastery making vodka for?
Certainly not for celibacy. Not here. Not this night.
Finished, before taking off,
he tosses the bottle out the window onto the beach.
It lays on the sand near the road, forgotten.
Sun fades the label.
Moon shines through the glass.
No one else seems to disturb it.
3 STAR Vodka. A Pint.

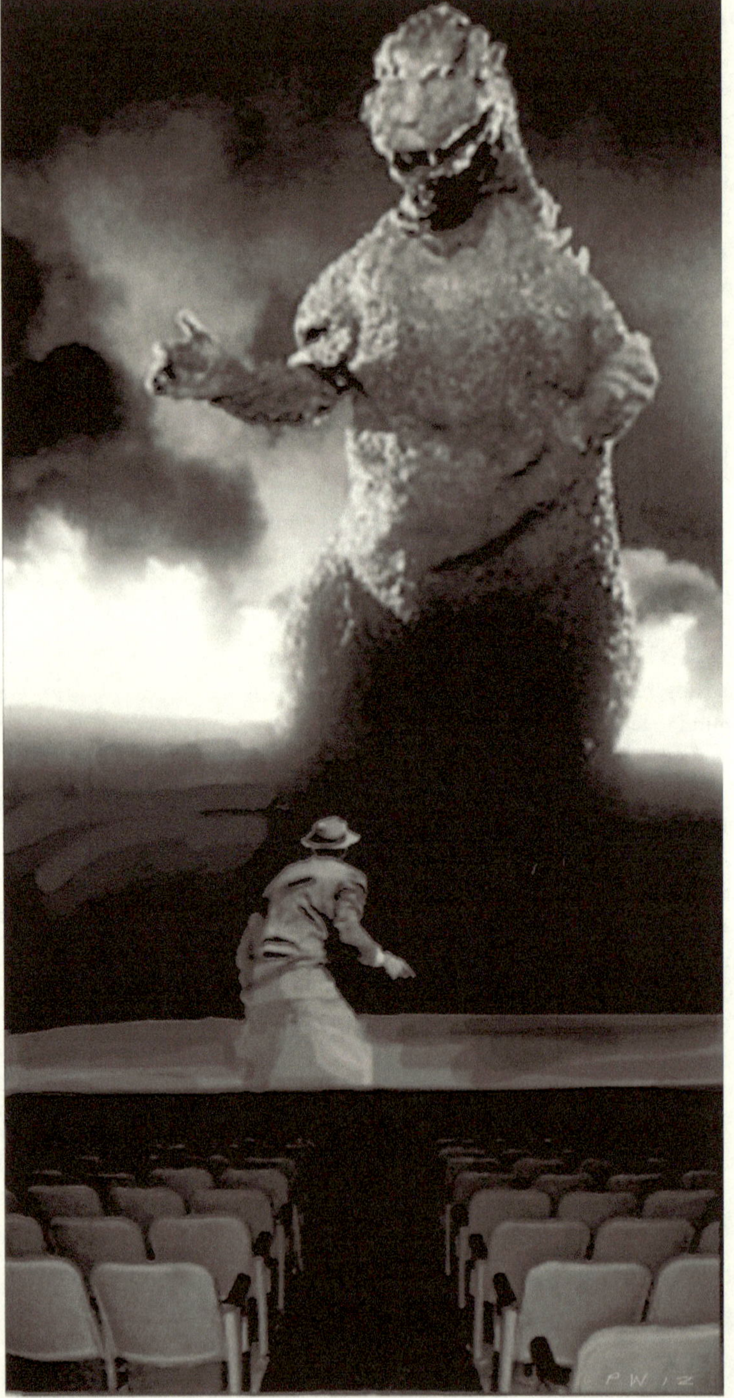
PW 12

Word That Escapes

Grandpa was a police officer.
He wasn't with us, maybe at the station, somewhere,
so Grandma and I go to the movies to kill time.
We sit in the dark.
Silhouettes of strangers in the rows ahead flash
in front of the moving black and white pictures on the screen.
We're inside the Palomar.
Its fancy hanging chandeliers, ornate decorative plaster,
and sumptuous velvet curtains
frame the spectacle screaming in front of us.
We're in a city. It's 1952.
This giant lizard is trashing everything in sight.
Flips its tail all over the place and steps on things, crushing them.
People name him Godzilla.
Occasionally he looks down at us.
He roars and lumbers forward.
People shriek. Run. We're like ants.
Then this policeman steps forward.
Unholstering his pistol, he aims and fires.
Continuing to unload, he pumps away. Fills Godzilla with lead
but in nothing flat Godzilla reaches down,
picks him up with his mouth,
his legs and arms jerking spasmodically from between teeth.
Doesn't even bat an eye, this Godzilla.
When lights come on we join others who sat there in the dark
cowering, even shivering, and shuffle hypnotically
up the sloping theater aisle carpet toward parted lobby curtains.
It's then that Grandma asks how I liked the movie.
I try to impress her with instant criticism, turning and telling her
just how stupid that dumb cop was, proud of my instant assessment.
I feel older than I am.
Suddenly, surprising me, through clenched teeth she says
Young man, I don't ever want to hear you say that word again.
That was a po-lice off-i-cer. Not a cop,
a po--lice off--i--cer, she says,
bitingly articulating each syllable.

About the Type

Minion is the name of the typeface that this book was set in. It was designed by Robert Slimbach in 1990 for Adobe Systems. A serif typeface, it was inspired by late Renaissance-era type. This typeface possesses a lowercase that is large in size in relation to its uppercase.

Of interest: Robert Bringhurst's *The Elements of Typographic Style* uses Minion as its body face. Stieg Larsson's *Millennium Triology* was set in this typeface. The trailer for Terrence Malick's *The Tree of Life* uses Minion for its credits. Haruki Murakami's *1Q84* uses the Minion typeface.

About the Author

Perry Woodfin has a Bachelor of Fine Arts degree from Washington State University, and has worked full time as an artist since 1965. As a lifelong resident of Washington State, the content of his art reflects the Northwest. The beauty of Northwest landscape, the common and ordinary things that exhibit history of use, the human themes of romance, pathos, comedy, and ritual, and his love of poetry, all show up in his art. "I try to capture and exhibit the force and spirit these things hold for me," he says. He lives and works on Whidbey Island, just north of Seattle.

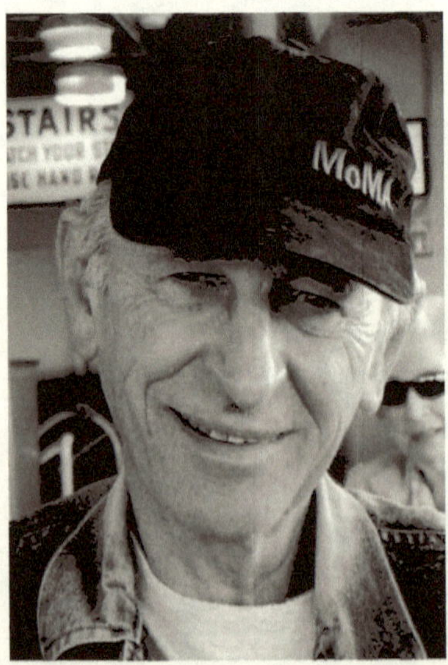

www.ingramcontent.com/pod-product-compliance
Lightning Source LLC
LaVergne TN
LVHW091009080826
845145LV00003B/1193

* 9 7 8 0 6 1 5 6 0 4 1 2 1 *